About Island Press

Island Press is the only nonprofit organization in the United States whose principal purpose is the publication of books on environmental issues and natural resource management. We provide solutions-oriented information to professionals, public officials, business and community leaders, and concerned citizens who are shaping responses to environmental problems.

In 2005, Island Press celebrates its twenty-first anniversary as the leading provider of timely and practical books that take a multidisciplinary approach to critical environmental concerns. Our growing list of titles reflects our commitment to bringing the best of an expanding body of literature to the environmental community throughout North America and the world.

Support for Island Press is provided by the Agua Fund, Brainerd Foundation, Geraldine R. Dodge Foundation, Doris Duke Charitable Foundation, Educational Foundation of America, The Ford Foundation, The George Gund Foundation, The William and Flora Hewlett Foundation, Henry Luce Foundation, The John D. and Catherine T. MacArthur Foundation, The Andrew W. Mellon Foundation, The Curtis and Edith Munson Foundation, National Environmental Trust, The New-Land Foundation, Oak Foundation, The Overbrook Foundation, The David and Lucile Packard Foundation, The Pew Charitable Trusts, The Rockefeller Foundation, The Winslow Foundation, and other generous donors.

The opinions expressed in this book are those of the author(s) and do not necessarily reflect the views of these foundations.

Sprawl Costs

Sprawl Costs

Economic Impacts of Unchecked Development

Robert W. Burchell
Anthony Downs
Barbara McCann
Sahan Mukherji

Washington · Covelo · London

Island Press is a trademark of The Center for Resource Economics.

Library of Congress Cataloging-in-Publication data.
Burchell, Robert W.
  Sprawl costs : economic impacts of unchecked development / Robert Burchell, Anthony Downs, Barbara McCann, and Sahan Mukherji.
      p. cm.
  Includes bibliographical references and index.
  ISBN 1-55963-570-3 (cloth : alk. paper) — ISBN 1-55963-530-4 (pbk. : alk. paper)
   1. Cities and towns—Growth—Economic aspects—United States.
2. Cities and towns—Growth—Environmental aspects—United States.
3. Suburbs—United States. 4. Real estate development—United States.
I. Downs, Anthony. II. Mukherji, Sahan. III. Title.
  HT384.U5B87 2005
  307.76'0973—dc22

                                                            2004029253

British Cataloguing-in-Publication data available.

Printed on recycled, acid-free paper ⊛

Design by Maureen Gately

Manufactured in the United States of America
10 9 8 7 6 5 4 3 2 1

Contents

Chapter 1

Aerial photograph of Las Vegas, Nevada. Photograph by Reid Ewing.

Introduction

CRITICS OF SUBURBAN SPRAWL maintain that the predominance of this growth form over the past fifty years has significantly harmed American society. They say that sprawl—the spread-out development of separated subdivisions, office parks, malls, and strip shopping centers growing beyond existing cities and towns—has thwarted public transit development, separated rich and poor, caused unnecessary travel, consumed fragile land, and generated excessive public expenditures. On the other side of the discussion, some believe that sprawl is as American as apple pie and that citizens are getting what they want: single-family homes on large lots, safe communities with good school systems, unrestricted automobile use, and metropolitan locations far from the pace and problems of urban areas. These and other benefits of sprawl, they argue, mean life is good. "If it ain't broke, don't fix it."

In fact, sprawl has been so well accepted by the public that the prime-rated locations for both residential and nonresidential development are located increasingly farther out rather than closer in and are more rather than less segregated by type of land use. Gated communities, farmettes, research parks, law offices, medical groups, mega-hardware and home improvement stores, theatrical and comedy clubs, new and used car lots, and restaurants all now seek peripheral locations in pursuit of their markets. The move to the far reaches of the metropolitan area began with single-family subdivisions; shopping centers and garden apartments sprang up next, then research and industrial parks, followed by restaurants and entertainment facilities, and finally, discounters of every form.

The unique aspect of all this development is that few entities have ever failed because their decisions to move outward were in the wrong direction. Occasionally, a retailer or a residential development has gone under because an exit on the interstate or beltway was not developed as planned, but rarely has an economic entity failed in the United States because it was developed too far out.

If sprawl is so desirable, why should the citizens of the United States accept anything else? The answer is that they no longer can pay for the infrastructure necessary to develop farther and farther out in metropolitan areas. The cost to provide public infrastructure and services in new sprawling development is higher than the cost to service that same population in a more compact development form. Sprawling, "leapfrog" developments require longer public roads and water and sewer lines to provide service. Water and sewer services constitute a large portion of the capital costs of new communities, whether they are paid for by the developer, the new home buyer, or the local government. Sprawl can inflate the costs of these new water and sewer hookups by 20 to 40 percent.

Sprawl creates a never-ending upward spiral of costs. Increased usage of city roads due to the increased population makes immediate improvements necessary. The city then has to provide services to the new area. Sprawling developments also impose higher costs on police and fire departments and schools. Not as readily apparent are the costs that a new development will impose on the municipality in years to come. In all likelihood, it will not generate enough property taxes to pay for the services it requires. Farther down the road, all of the new infrastructure, originally paid for by the developer, will need maintenance and repair.

As the suburbs on the fringe struggle with the costs of building new infrastructure and schools, cities and older suburbs struggle with another set of costs as development leaves them behind: the costs of urban decline and a concentration of poverty. Sprawling development has helped concentrate poor households in cities, often far from the new jobs being created in the suburbs. City and inner-suburban governments are burdened with the increased costs of taking care of poor households and repairing aging infrastructure, even as they lose middle-class taxpayers.

A fundamental characteristic of sprawl is that two sets of infrastructure are being created that are both underused: the one that Americans have been running away from (cities and older developed suburbs) and the one they never catch up with (the new sprawling development). This ever-expanding pattern of development results in overly high costs to local governments, developers, and home buyers and renters. A look at one state brings the picture into sharper focus. In South Carolina, if sprawl continues unchecked, statewide infrastructure costs for the period 1995 to 2015 are projected to be more than $56 billion, or $750 per citizen per year for these twenty years. Roads would cost 2.5 times what would be spent on primary, secondary, and higher education infrastructure; three times what would be spent on health infrastructure, including all hospitals, institutions, and water-sewer treatment systems; ten times what would be spent on public safety, administration, and justice infrastructure; fifteen times what would be spent on environmental protection infrastructure; and twenty-five times what would be spent on all cultural and recreational infrastructure.

In addition to a massive infrastructure conservation program and the adoption of numerous technological cost savers, funding this infrastructure in South Carolina would require an increase in the gasoline tax of 2 cents per gallon, the tolling of all interstates at thirty-mile intervals, and an increase in property taxes of 12.5 percent.

The costs of sprawling development take on a particular relevance against the backdrop of acute state and local fiscal troubles. State governments have been facing some of the toughest economic conditions in decades due to the recent recession, declines in federal support, and rising costs, particularly in health care.[1] City governments are also facing a squeeze; many states have withdrawn significant local financial support to local governments, and health care and wage costs are soaring.[2] City managers also cite infrastructure costs as a primary place where costs are rising: 65 percent say rising infrastructure costs are negatively affecting the ability of their budget to meet the city's needs.[3] Many state and local governments are raising taxes to balance their budgets.

It is possible to accommodate growth in another way: be more centrally focused in development patterns and consume fewer resources when development takes place. This type of compact development allows all development that would have taken place under sprawl growth to occur, but it directs that development to locations where public services can be provided more efficiently. Its more compact form gives more people the option to travel via foot, bicycle, or transit, easing the burden on the road network. Both factors allow appreciable savings in a relatively short time. Resources need not be as aggressively consumed, yet the amount of residential and nonresidential development is not altered.

Further, growth that emphasizes reinvestment and prosperity in the urban core may have the power to enhance not just the overall competitiveness of a region but the economic health of all of its parts. A growing literature of urban-suburban "interdependence" finds that boosting central city income growth and reducing core poverty improve overall metropolitan area income growth.

Costs need to be measured in terms of not just capital improvement but also resource depletion. Land in the United States is being consumed at triple the rate of household formation, automobile use is growing twice as fast as the population, and prime agricultural land, forests, and fragile lands encompassing natural habitats are decreasing at comparable reciprocal rates. Many "costs" to individuals are hard to quantify; for example, individuals "pay" for traffic congestion with their time. New evidence even indicates that sprawling development may increase health care costs by making it more difficult for people to get the physical activity essential for health.

Still, an alternative to the current pattern of land development is by no means the ultimate panacea. Returning to our South Carolina example, if the state switched to compact development and managed growth measures to curtail sprawl development, it would save only about 10 percent of the projected $56 billion in infrastructure costs, or approximately $5.6 billion. This is because about 40 percent of public infrastructure costs are not growth related and only about two-thirds of the remainder is *new* growth related. When development pattern savings are applied to the appropriate portion of new growth–related infrastructure costs, the savings are only 12 to 15 percent.

On the other hand, increasing the gasoline tax by 2 cents per gallon, a politically risky measure, raises only $56 million in new revenues statewide—one one-thousandth of the total required infrastructure costs, and one one-hundredth of the amount that potentially could be saved by altering land development patterns.

In sum, the majority of the American public is not unhappy with the current pattern of development in metropolitan areas—it simply can no longer afford it. Thus, the primary concern about sprawl development, at a time when the average American is satisfied with its outcome, is *cost*.

Whatever form growth takes in the future, it is sure to occur. About every five years for the last several decades, the United States added 10 to 12 million people in 5 million housing units. By one estimate, over the next thirty years the United States is expected to become home to 90 million new people, most of them in metropolitan areas. According to an analysis by Arthur C. Nelson at Virginia Tech, that means we will need to build 40 million new homes and replace 20 million aging homes. We will produce 60 million new jobs, which will require 50 billion more square feet to support workers; another 40 billion square feet of commercial space will also have to be replaced. In all, Nelson predicts that the United States will need 217 billion square feet of new or rejuvenated space in the next thirty years. That is about 75 percent of all the development on the ground today.[4] Clearly, the question of how the nation grows—and how much it will cost—is critical.

Measuring the Costs of Sprawl

While the benefits of smarter growth may seem obvious, the actual costs of sprawl have remained elusive. In 1974, in the first attempt to quantify those costs, the Real Estate Research Corporation published *The Costs of Sprawl*. In its more than one thousand pages, the study laid out how and why sprawling low-density development is more expensive than compact forms of development. Regarded by the social science community as one of the most significant critiques of sprawl and among the most influential studies ever undertaken, *The Costs of Sprawl* has been cited in countless environmental and planning reports and journals, reviewed—both positively and negatively—by more than one hundred journals and magazines, and presented as the seminal study on growth impacts to numerous congressional committees and bodies.

Although *The Costs of Sprawl* has been influential, it is also flawed. Critics have discounted its results for several reasons. One of the most serious is that the researchers allowed the size of homes and the number of occupants to vary in the different community types. Critics say this means that the absence of sprawl was not the reason for much of the cost savings; rather, smaller units and fewer people to service were the cause of the savings. Yet, even though these and other shortcomings have been uncovered, the direction of the findings so paralleled past and current intuitive feelings that the study continues to be used today as one of the most cogent arguments against sprawled development patterns.

The "costs" of sprawl have been talked about for decades, often without a full understanding of what these costs are and to what level they should be assigned. In the original *Costs of Sprawl* study, costs were calculated in six different substantive areas and assigned to the community, to the individual, and to society as a whole. Infrastructure and transportation costs were assigned to the community; housing and quality-of-life costs, to the individual; and energy and environmental costs, both to the community and to society as a whole. While this assignment is somewhat arbitrary, it is a characteristic of the sprawl literature that continues today. Most cost-accounting efforts assign sprawl costs to either the easiest or the most common level of measurement.

Other studies in the years since have documented the costs of sprawl on a smaller scale, at the state, metropolitan, or even community level; the results of some of these studies will be referenced later. One set of complementary research has focused narrowly on comparing the costs of providing community services with the taxes brought in by various land uses, concluding that suburban housing developments do not bring in the taxes to support the services they require. Many of these studies have been sponsored by the American Farmland Trust, which uses them to demonstrate that working farms can "pay their own way."[5]

In 2002, the National Research Council published *The Costs of Sprawl—2000*, a massive research document meant to update and improve on the seminal *Costs of Sprawl* study from 1974. The study set out two different futures for the United States—one of low-density sprawl development at the outer reaches of the metropolitan area, and the other of more compact, smarter development—and compared their differing impacts on land, infrastructure, housing costs, and public services. It quantified the potential costs of sprawl over the next twenty-five years while also acknowledging its benefits. This book is in large part based on the findings of that study. The results should provide policy makers and citizens with credible evidence that the costs of sprawl, while perhaps not as extreme as projected by some analysts, are enough to merit a shift toward more compact, efficient development.

No exploration of the costs of sprawl would be complete without also discussing the benefits of this development pattern. These benefits generally mirror costs. They involve resource gains attributable to type of development pattern. Such gains may involve, for example, monetary gains due to reduced housing costs from building farther out, shorter suburb-to-suburb travel time because most residences and jobs are now suburban, or such social gains as the ability to achieve homeownership, again due to location in more distant places.

The purpose of this book is to provide a reasonable amount of evidence on the costs of sprawl as well as the potential savings as a function of more compact growth. The benefits of sprawl cannot be discounted in attempting to provide a blueprint for future action. Taking both costs and benefits into account, it makes sense to attempt a more planned and resource-conserving growth strategy for the future. The rationale behind this decision is contained in the following chapters.

Increasingly, the linkages among resource conservation, planned growth, economic development, and quality of life are being made clear, and the answers are pointing us in a common direction. It makes resource, economic, fiscal, and market sense to be careful about where and how we grow. This common purpose will lead to a more sustainable U.S. society.

Chapter 2

Aerial photograph of Albuquerque, New Mexico. Photograph by Reid Ewing.

Sprawl and Its Definition

ALEXIS DE TOCQUEVILLE, touring the United States in the early 1800s, marveled at "America ... where everything is in constant motion ... and where no boundaries were set to the efforts of man." Today's sprawl is akin to the frontier of long ago and to the postwar suburb, both of which have been extolled as defining American influences.

The term *sprawl* has taken on a pejorative as well as a descriptive connotation, an intermixing that makes a balanced discussion difficult. For Americans who have grown up knowing nothing else, the spread of urban areas and the destruction of open space that sprawl brings may seem inevitable. But sprawl is a type of development with several key characteristics—and these traits are what make it so costly. The three traits used to define sprawl here include (1) unlimited outward extension into undeveloped areas, (2) low density, and (3) leapfrog development. Sprawl also includes strict segregation of housing and commercial development, often through the construction of standardized development types, automobile dependence, and fragmented planning and governance.

The first of sprawl's distinct characteristics is its significant consumption of exurban agricultural and other frail lands. New developments are built beyond the metropolitan core, commonly in areas with limited infrastructure or public services. Agricultural acreage is lost because it often is the cheapest land available for development. Fragile environmental lands are swallowed up because they are part of the otherwise developable tracts.

Another element in the cardinal definition of sprawl is density, or more specifically, low density. But density has to be set in context; densities in the United States overall are roughly one-tenth what they are in Western Europe; in turn, Western European density is much lower than that of Japan and only a fraction of what is found in such locations as Hong Kong and Indonesia. In all of these locations, suburban densities are lower than the densities of central cities. Sprawl is not simply development at less-than-maximum density; rather, it refers to development at a low *relative* density, and one that may be too costly to maintain.

Sprawl also refers to a particular type of peripheral growth that expands by leapfrogging outward from the solidly built up core of a metropolitan area. Sprawling developments may be built in isolated areas, creating a patchwork in which working farms are right next to suburban housing developments, or in which shopping malls border open fields.

These three traits form the basis for our examination of the costs of sprawl, but other characteristics are also important and play a role in sprawl's impact, even if they are more difficult to measure in a national study. In sprawl, development usually occurs in strictly defined forms. Residential development contains primarily single-family housing, including suburban subdivisions and significant numbers of individual homes scattered in outlying areas. Nonresidential development includes shopping centers, strip retail outlets along arterial roads, big box stores, industrial and office parks, and freestanding industrial and office buildings as well as schools and other public buildings. In fact, one reason sprawl is so prevalent is that these well-defined development types can be reproduced anywhere with predictable results, thus reducing risk to developers and the banks that finance them.

Another familiar characteristic of sprawl is that these different development types are spatially segregated. Homes are built only next to other homes, and strip malls next to strip malls. Development practices, and often zoning codes, mean that within each zoning district, only one type of use usually is permitted—for example, single-family residential, shopping centers, or office parks. Separation is such a fundamental characteristic that when two different uses are next to each other, a berm or other barrier is sometimes constructed between them.

Under sprawl conditions, the separation of uses and leapfrog development create an almost total reliance on the automobile to meet daily needs. Automobile travel has helped to shape sprawl, as the growth of an extensive network of local highways and federally funded interstate freeways provided access to areas away from the downtown core. The automobile is the most efficient means of accessing sprawl's outward extension and skipped-over development; most suburban areas have extremely poor or nonexistent transit access, and bicycling or walking is simply impractical in many areas. For seven-day-a-week business and recreational use, including both at-peak and off-peak use, nothing can match the automobile for cost, efficiency, and versatility—at least in the short term. The road system itself has become inextricably linked to sprawl: instead of traditional street grids, sprawling areas usually have a hierarchical road system in which cul-de-sacs feed into subdivision streets, which feed into arterial roads that connect the separated land uses.

Some analysts also include fragmented governance and a lack of integrated land use planning as important aspects of suburban sprawl. They point to the strong influence of small developers, who can create relatively small residential subdivisions and nonresidential site plans while operating independently of one another within the zoning districts of the eighteen thousand local governments found throughout the United States. The legal framework within which sprawl occurs is fragmented into numerous relatively small units, separately controlled by discrete local governments with unique rules and regulations. These localities have different fiscal resources; some are quite wealthy, whereas others have limited ability to pay for local services. The poorer localities are at a severe disadvantage when competing for development.

In sum, for the purposes of building a national profile of sprawling versus nonsprawling development, *sprawl* is defined as significant development in a relatively pristine setting: rural or undeveloped counties. In nearly every instance, this development is low density, it has leapt over other development to become established in an outlying area, and its very location indicates that it is unbounded.

The Origins of Sprawl

Sprawling development provides certain benefits. Home buyers with less to spend find they can "drive until they qualify," finding lower-cost housing at the edge of metropolitan areas. Sprawl can dilute congestion while accommodating unlimited use of the automobile. It distances new development from the fiscal and social problems of older core areas while allowing residents to live in economically homogeneous areas in which crime is perceived to be lower and houses are expected to appreciate steadily. Suburban schools provide both education and appropriate socialization for youth while requiring lower property taxes than city schools.

Preservation of these benefits is behind some of the laws and regulations that now encourage sprawling growth. While sprawl is typically believed to be a result of market forces expressing consumer preferences, in fact a web of local zoning ordinances, state policies, and federal laws and programs has encouraged sprawl to such a degree that it is often difficult to build anything else. The growth of sprawl has its genesis in the post–World War II push by federal and state policies to promote the growth of the suburbs. The federal mortgage interest income tax deduction encouraged home ownership—and the new federal mortgage loan program established in 1949 guaranteed new construction while encouraging economic and racial segregation. Floodplain insurance made it easier to build in outlying areas. The federal interstate highway program, begun in 1956, provided local communities with 90 percent of the funds needed to build interstate highways, including perimeter roads around major cities that ended up serving as major commuting corridors. Historically low gasoline prices helped things along, and racial integration in the 1960s and 1970s encouraged "white flight" from the cities. At the local level, zoning that strictly segregated uses and mandated accommodation of the automobile with extensive parking became the norm. All of these policies and trends ignored the needs of existing areas, and many of the policies made it difficult to renovate or rebuild in urban areas.

While all these forces encouraged sprawl, government entities have at the same time had a limited ability to direct development. John Delafons, author of *Land-Use Controls in the United States,* describes the U.S. system of master planning, zoning, and subdivision control as heavily influenced by a "prairie psychology."[1] U.S. development controls are "static" and thus lack the ability to control the tempo (timing) and sequence (which location first) of development. Development is free to wander and to take place incrementally in jurisdictions in the United States because existing land use controls allow this to happen.

Largely as a result of these policies, the shift to the suburbs has been manifest for more than half a century. In 1940, only 15 percent of the U.S. population resided in the suburbs (defined as metropolitan areas outside of central cities). Sixty years later, about 60 percent of the population was counted as suburban. The amount of land consumed by sprawl increased by one-half from 1950 to 1980, and by one-half again from 1980 to 2000.

Even the suburbs are now being bypassed by development seeking locations at the fringe of metropolitan areas. The newest and soon to be one of the most successful airports in the United States is thirty-three miles from the city of Denver, Colorado; a taxi ride from the airport baggage claim to the downtown Hyatt costs $40. Is this an anomaly? No. Cincinnati's new airport is so far from downtown that it is not even in the same state! Both airports have already attracted nonresidential development and are now drawing residential development to their edges. Both are tens of miles from the nearest existing development of these types. But neither can justify its location solely on flight pattern interference with residential environments. Instead, the locations were chosen for exactly the same reason other land use locations are chosen: an abundance of land was available, and it was both relatively inexpensive and easy to assemble.

Alternatives to Sprawl

What is the alternative to this endless spread of development? Some might say you need look no further than the site of Denver's old airport, Stapleton. Developers have recycled 1,100 acres of runways and are now building "an urban tapestry" of homes, shops, and offices just five miles east of downtown Denver. With plans for more than twelve thousand houses and apartments, three thousand square feet of retail space, and ten thousand square feet of offices, the new, masterplanned Stapleton is being designed as a walkable community where residents can meet daily needs without getting in an automobile. The

FIGURE 2.1: Mixed-use development in Princeton, New Jersey. Photograph by Catherine Galley.

new development also is designed to integrate with the existing residential neighborhoods that surround it.

Smart growth advocates promote mixing land uses, directing development toward existing communities, using compact building design, and preserving open space and farmland. They encourage the creation of a range of housing and transportation choices, walkable communities, and a strong sense of place. Because these principles are intended to solve many ills, controlling costs may not be the primary goal of many smart growth advocates. For this analysis, we look not at the whole realm of smart growth techniques but at a more limited set of controlled growth measures that are primarily aimed at focusing development in already built up areas.

The Future of Growth

As the United States looks to the future, what type of growth will predominate? Even the most vehement critics of sprawl recognize that these suburban and exurban growth patterns will continue in the United States. The laws, policies, and programs that have encouraged sprawling development are still in place and are unlikely to be changed overnight. The recent population increase of 20 to 30 million people per decade is likely to continue for at least the next quarter century. As the children of the baby boomers age, they will be moving from condominiums into larger homes to raise their children —and the size of the average new home is now twice what it was in 1970. The building industry will most likely continue to use highway access as a primary criterion in constructing commercial developments. As a result, skipped-over development will continue to occur in rural and undeveloped areas. It would be unrealistic to expect growth to occur solely in already built up neighborhoods in cities or in close-by inner suburbs.

But the potential for more compact growth is also strong. From 2000 to 2010, half the net population growth is projected to be baby boomers aging into their fifties, many of whom are ready to give up single-family homes and move into more compact housing with more destinations close by. The number of children under the age of five is expected to remain fairly steady, and surveys show that households with children prefer sidewalks, smaller lots, and higher-density housing. An analysis conducted for the Congress for the New Urbanism predicts that 30 to 55 percent of new households may prefer dense walkable neighborhoods by the end of this decade.[2] At the same time, successful mixed-use developments are emerging both in existing urban areas and in exurban new communities, opening the door for more such developments.

It may be that the next stage in the nation's settlement patterns will focus development in already established centers. Most important when looking at costs, even a modest shift of development back to core areas, combined with more-compact growth in outlying areas, could consume far less capital and fewer natural resources. In many cases, redirecting just 20 percent of the growth headed for areas outside central cities and inner suburbs would double or triple the growth projected for these inner areas.[3]

The next chapter of this book begins our look into the future by laying out two different development scenarios—one of continued sprawl, the other of more compact growth. While the actual number of potential futures for the United States is infinite, these two scenarios provide a clear picture of the financial consequences of continued sprawling development and of the benefits of choosing a more carefully planned and compact form of development.

Chapter 3

Single-family subdivision in Manheim, Pennsylvania. Photograph by Anton Nelessen.

Measuring Sprawl
in the United States

As of 2000, the United States was a country of 281 million people living in 103 million households, holding 159 million jobs, and earning $6.4 trillion in annual income (see Table 3.1). Over the period 2000 to 2025, population in the United States is expected to grow by 61 million, the number of households by 24 million, employment by 49 million, and annual income by $4 trillion.[1] A large concentration of the nation's significant growth, whatever its form, is expected to take place in a relatively small number of geographic areas. Three of fifty states, 10 of 172 regions, and 40 of nearly 3,100 counties will contain one-third of the nation's household growth through 2025. Every list of the fastest-growing states, regions, and counties is dominated by entries from the South and West regions. Together, the South and West will represent about 80 percent of future population and household growth and nearly 70 percent of future employment and income growth.

Building Scenarios for Growth

What form will all this growth take, and how much will it cost? In attempting to answer this question, this book builds two plausible future growth scenarios for the entire United States and compares

TABLE 3.1
United States Growth in Population, Number of Households, Employment, and Income, 2000–2025

	Population	Households	Jobs	Income
Year 2000	281,422,000	103,245,000	159,390,000	$6,350,428,000,000
Year 2025	342,150,000	126,699,000	208,808,000	$10,352,391,000,000
Growth	60,728,000	23,454,000	49,418,000	$4,001,963,000,000
Growth rate	21.6%	22.7%	31%	63%

Source: U.S. Department of Commerce, Bureau of the Census (2000). Projection data from Woods & Poole (1998). Data interpretation by the Center for Urban Policy Research, Rutgers University.

their costs. These scenarios are based on careful evaluation of existing data about where development exists and what form it takes. Using modeling techniques, current patterns are projected into the future, according to either a sprawling or a compact growth scenario. With much of the data coming from the U.S. Census, the results of this modeling can be evaluated at the regional, state, metropolitan, and county levels. Where costs are calculated, 2000 year dollars have been used. This chapter provides an explanation of how the models were built and what they show about where and how the United States can be expected to grow.

Models looking into the future have their limitations. They cannot take into account the dynamic "learning" process that may result in the gradual adoption of smart growth techniques. It can also be difficult to separate the results from the assumptions made to build the model. Finally, the "irrational" decisions made by local governments, the happenstance of the real world that affects costs, simply cannot be captured. However, these models do help us see patterns in future development, and they provide insight into the broad impact that development decisions may have in the future.[2] It is also important to note that the costs—and the savings—projected in this study apply to the accommodation of *growth:* the new residents and new structures expected to become part of the United States over the next twenty-five years. The study does not account for changes to land use patterns that affect current residents.

Measuring Sprawl

The first challenge lies simply in measuring current development patterns and the degree of sprawl. Some components of sprawl are not easily measured. For example, although it is possible to track residential single-family and nonresidential commercial and retail development taking place at low densities in the United States and accessed by automobiles in rural and undeveloped areas, this is the point at which almost all tracking stops. Measures of leapfrog development, or development that is spatially segregated, are virtually impossible. Measures of how much development is being delivered by small developers in local jurisdictions are achievable but generally are unproductive. Finally, although a measure of gross residential density (number of dwelling units divided by area of jurisdiction) is readily available, this gross measure often masks the actual land takings of individual new developments.

Despite these challenges, a number of indices have been created to measure sprawl. Prime among these are those developed by the Rutgers University Center for Urban Policy Research (CUPR), Smart Growth America, and *USA Today*. The Smart Growth America and *USA Today* indices are static measures of sprawl—that is, how much of past growth is sprawl. Of these two static indices, the Smart Growth America index is the more comprehensive, measuring sprawl in terms of density, the integration or mix of homes with commercial or other uses, the strength of urban and town centers, and the degree to which the streets provide multiple well-connected routes. However, this index covers a limited number of metropolitan areas. The *USA Today* index covers most of the United States but depicts sprawl in a much more limited way, evaluating density and the percentage of each metropolitan area contained within its U.S. Census–defined urbanized area: the smaller the percentage, the more sprawl that occurs.

In contrast, the Rutgers classification, on which this book is based, is a dynamic index of how much of past growth is sprawl and how much of future growth is likely to be sprawl. This enables geographic areas to be categorized as sustained, growing, or declining sprawl areas. The Rutgers index also allows for geographies other than metropolitan areas to be viewed as sprawling. The purpose of defining sprawl as a type of growth is to be able to assess the future costs of pursuing this strategy versus pursuing a more compact form of future growth.

One of the most difficult tasks of all of these analyses is, in fact, to define sprawl, due to both the complexity of the concept and the limitations of the data available. The Rutgers study defines sprawl by three principal characteristics (discussed in Chapter 2): unlimited outward extension, low density, and leapfrog development. Even though areas that are already sprawling exist, the Rutgers index focuses on the impacts of future sprawl versus alternative development.

Central to the definition of sprawl employed in the Rutgers index is rapid and significant growth in rural and undeveloped counties. Since growth is a relative concept, the study determined each county's growth rate in relation to its Economic Area. The Economic Area (EA) is a geographic area defined by the U.S. Department of Commerce that groups major metropolitan areas with their associated rural and undeveloped counties. These areas are typically much larger than the more familiar Metropolitan Statistical Areas (MSAs) and Consolidated Metropolitan Statistical Areas (CMSAs), but they allow an evaluation of rural counties in relation to their closest metropolitan centers. This classification covers the entire United States and allows an evaluation of the large areas as whole economic units. The United States is divided into 172 EAs, which include all 3,091 counties in the country.[3]

For the Rutgers study, sprawl was defined as taking place in nonurban locations (rural and undeveloped counties) where counties are experiencing very high growth rates. The emphasis on development in outlying areas means the model does not count a suburban-style housing subdivision built in an already developed area as sprawl. However, as a rule, most such single-use development tends to take place in outlying areas, while more mixed-use and compact development tends to take place in existing areas. Yet the separation of housing from other destinations, automobile dependence, and a lack of coordinated planning in such a subdivision remain important, and their impact is discussed when appropriate.

Where Sprawl Is Expected

According to the Rutgers sprawl index, 742 of 3,091 U.S. counties, or 24 percent, are expected to experience significant sprawl over the period 2000 to 2025. Of the 742 sprawl counties, 598 are rural and undeveloped counties and 144 are suburban and rural center counties. Proportionately, sprawl is expected to occur in 22 percent of rural and undeveloped counties and 54 percent of suburban and rural center counties. While sprawl development may be a significant presence in only one-quarter of U.S. counties, it will involve 13.1 million of the 23.5 million new households during the period 2000 to 2025. If current trends continue, sprawl is expected to involve 56 percent of all future household growth in the United States.

Figure 3.1 shows the counties that are projected to sprawl in the United States through 2025. Under the sprawl scenario, the most sprawl is expected to occur in ten western and southern states: Florida, California, Arizona, Texas, North Carolina, South Carolina, Colorado, Washington, Georgia, and Nevada. These ten states represent 58 percent of sprawl household growth nationwide, and 60 percent of nationwide household growth. One-eighth of all future sprawl growth is expected to take place in Florida. Of the ten states listed above, the share of overall growth that is sprawling is highest in Arizona, at nearly 98 percent, and lowest in Texas, at about 31 percent.

Sprawl of any significance is clearly happening in areas of the United States where growth is taking place. This does not mean, however, that sprawl is not taking place where there is no growth. Sprawl is occurring even in areas with no net growth. It is typically moving from the central city to the periphery of the metropolitan area even though the metropolitan area may be declining. Sprawl is found

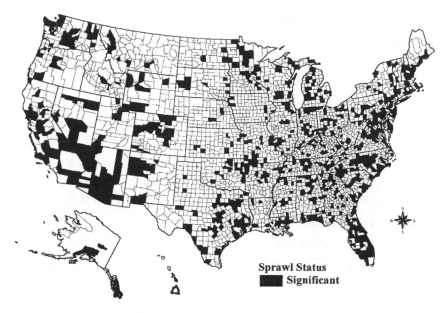

FIGURE 3.1: Projected sprawl in the United States: sprawl growth scenario.

in every facet of growth in the United States. Low-density, single-use, skipped-over development is found inside urban growth boundaries (e.g., Lexington, Kentucky), in the redevelopment areas of major cities (Newark, New Jersey), and in freestanding growth centers (Greenville-Spartanburg, South Carolina). Sprawl can also be evaluated at the regional level. Of the 172 Economic Areas in the United States, almost all are expected to experience some degree of sprawl; 156 EAs, or about 90 percent, are expected to have at least one sprawling county (the average is five). Again on a regional basis, sprawl is most prevalent in the South. It is found in 70 of 74, or 95 percent, of the South's EAs. Sprawl in the Midwest, the West, and the Northeast is expected to occur in about 88 percent of all Economic Areas.

The EAs expected to experience the greatest amount of sprawl are Phoenix–Mesa, Arizona; Los Angeles–Riverside, California; Miami–Ft. Lauderdale, Florida; Washington, DC–Baltimore; Denver–Boulder, Colorado; and Las Vegas, Nevada. The above findings confirm that significant sprawl is associated with significant growth.

Sprawl is a phenomenon characteristic of the fastest-growing states and regions of the United States, clearly pointing out the reality that no area is able to statistically contain its outward development.

Creating a Compact Growth Scenario

Once areas are defined as sprawling, how can growth be managed to provide better futures for these areas? In creating the compact growth scenario, growth was managed by limiting a significant share of development to already developed counties or to areas as close to those already developed as possible. This can be achieved in two ways. The first method limited the amount of growth taking place in the outer counties by redirecting it to inner counties. This was done by drawing the equivalent of an urban growth boundary around the developed counties and by allowing only a portion of the growth to go to the less developed counties (intercounty sprawl development).

The second method of controlling sprawl in a region (Economic Area) limited the outward movement of growth in a single county (intracounty sprawl development). This was accomplished by establishing an urban service area in a county and containing most of the growth within that service area. In the second method, a boundary was drawn around the existing concentration of growth in a county. This was often the U.S. Census–defined urbanized area. The rest of the county was "protected" from significant development because public services were not available there. These two methods of control form the compact growth scenario.

Under the compact growth scenario, household and job growth in sprawling counties is expected to be redirected to other, more developed counties within the region, if these counties can absorb such growth. The objective is to significantly reduce the amount of residential and nonresidential growth occurring in sprawling locations (rural, undeveloped, developing suburban, and developing rural center counties), reducing growth by one-quarter or more (see Figure 3.2).

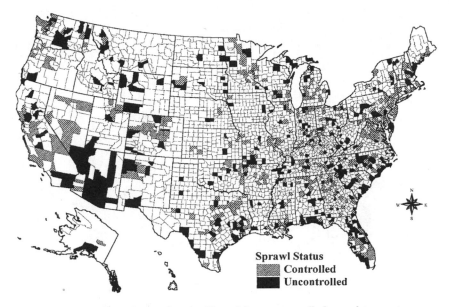

FIGURE 3.2: Projected sprawl in the United States: controlled growth scenario.

Every metropolitan region cannot simply draw urban growth and urban service boundaries to control sprawl. In fact, moving to more compact development patterns is a complex process, and many states and metropolitan areas are already engaging in dozens of innovative techniques that range from policy solutions to incentives to zoning changes. The model is useful in that it provides a systematic way to look at growth across the entire United States and to calculate the potential costs associated with that growth. It provides valuable information about the projected benefits of compact development, but it should not be taken as a policy prescription.

Comparing Sprawl and Compact Growth Scenarios

Both development alternatives involve growth that produces 53 million residential and nonresidential development units nationwide (26.49 million homes, 26.48 million nonresidential) over the twenty-five-year period 2000 to 2025. Approximately 23 million of these

TABLE 3.2

A. Development Units (Residential and Nonresidential) in Urban/Suburban/Rural Center Counties Versus Rural/Undeveloped Counties Sprawl and Compact Growth Scenarios, 2000–2025

Region	Sprawl Growth Scenario			Compact Growth Scenario			Difference in Urban/Suburban/Rural Center
	Urban/Suburban/Rural Center	Rural/Undeveloped	Total	Urban/Suburban/Rural Center	Rural/Undeveloped	Total	
Northeast	3,047,573	1,741,658	4,789,231	3,249,138	1,441,800	4,690,938	201,565
Midwest	5,660,869	3,617,810	9,278,679	5,868,049	3,294,885	9,162,934	207,180
South	14,012,671	8,898,927	22,911,598	15,233,613	7,510,753	22,744,366	1,220,942
West	10,825,683	5,162,439	15,988,122	12,306,686	3,564,868	15,871,554	1,481,003
United States	33,546,796	19,420,834	52,967,630	36,657,486	15,812,306	52,469,792	3,110,690

B. Population (age 16 and over) in Urban/Suburban/Rural Center Counties Versus Rural/Undeveloped Counties Sprawl and Compact Growth Scenarios, 2000–2025

Region	Sprawl Growth Scenario			Compact Growth Scenario			Difference in Urban/Suburban/Rural Center
	Urban/Suburban/Rural Center	Rural/Undeveloped	Total	Urban/Suburban/Rural Center	Rural/Undeveloped	Total	
Northeast	1,809,856	1,395,252	3,205,108	1,878,245	1,226,287	3,104,532	68,389
Midwest	3,912,127	3,040,529	6,952,655	4,142,550	2,786,972	6,929,522	230,424
South	13,783,357	8,371,645	22,155,001	14,620,750	7,481,196	22,101,946	837,393
West	10,493,288	5,666,584	16,159,872	11,976,576	4,360,059	16,336,636	1,483,289
United States	29,998,627	18,474,009	48,472,636	32,618,121	15,854,515	48,472,636	2,619,495

Source: Woods & Poole (1998); Center for Urban Policy Research, Rutgers University.

combined residential and nonresidential development units will be in the South, 16 million in the West, 9.3 million in the Midwest, and 4.8 million in the Northeast.

In the traditional, or sprawl development, scenario, of the 53 million development units, 33.6 million will be in urban and suburban counties and 19.4 million will be in rural and undeveloped counties. In the compact growth scenario resulting from shifting growth among counties, 36.7 million development units will be built in urban and suburban counties and 15.8 million will be built in rural and undeveloped counties. This represents a shift of 3.1 million development units to the more urban and suburban locations on a base of 33.6 million, a shift of more than 9.2 percent (Table 3.2a).

Under the compact growth scenario, an additional 2 million development units would be relocated within their county to more developed areas. These development units are projected to be built at 20 percent higher density, or a 10 percent increase in floor-area ratio (FAR). In the undeveloped areas under the same scenario, about 20 percent of the residential units are projected to be developed in cluster developments where density is twice as high as the prevailing density of undeveloped areas. In addition, one-quarter more housing units are developed as townhomes or multifamily buildings rather than as single-family detached or mobile home units.

This redirection of households and employment to more developed counties is projected to significantly reduce sprawl in 420 (57 percent) of the 742 sprawling counties. Thus, in a perfect world, only 420 of 740 counties whose sprawl was significant could be controlled if an urban growth boundary were introduced within the Economic Area containing these counties.

Another way to look at this shift is in terms of where residents will live under the two growth scenarios. With sprawl, nearly 62 percent of new residents age 16 and over—30 million people—will live in developed places, including urban, suburban, and counties with a rural center; 18.5 million new residents will live in undeveloped counties. An urban growth boundary would mean that the number of people living in developed places would increase slightly to 32.6 million people, or approximately 67 percent of new residents, while the number in undeveloped counties would be expected to drop to 15.9 million (Table 3.2b). Under the compact growth scenario, approximately 2.6 million people would move from less developed to more developed counties. The designation of county urban service areas would result in a shift of another 1.8 million people from the undeveloped to the developed portions of the counties where they were already expected to reside. In total, based on the model used in this analysis, 4.4 million people are expected to shift where they live.

Examples

The best way to illustrate how these models were constructed is to look at the scenarios built for specific regions. Each region has a unique sprawl profile. The following examples show the range in the degree of sprawl and in the ability to contain it through the techniques used in the model.

ATLANTA

Atlanta has become the commercial, transportation, and cultural capital of the southeastern United States. Its Economic Area ranks in the top ten for total growth and for sprawling development. Of the sixty-seven counties considered to be under its economic influence, twenty are expected to be sprawling; most of these are second-ring counties around Atlanta, including Carroll, Fayette, Henry, and Rockdale counties. Six counties are urban or suburban counties that are expected to be able to accept more growth. These include DeKalb and Fulton counties, which encompass the city of Atlanta; Clayton, Cobb, and Gwinnett counties; and Clarke County, which contains the city of Athens to the east.

Figure 3.3a shows the counties in Atlanta that are expected to sprawl. Figure 3.3b shows that if some growth were controlled and redirected to the six counties best able to absorb it, most counties

(a)

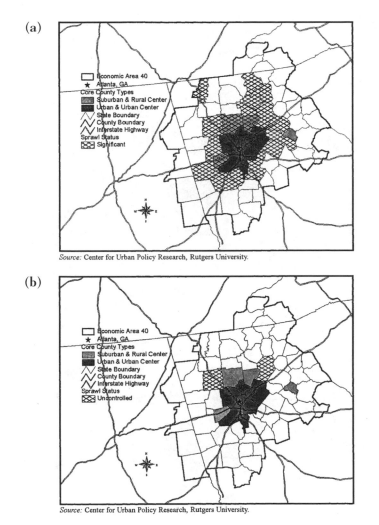

Source: Center for Urban Policy Research, Rutgers University.

(b)

Source: Center for Urban Policy Research, Rutgers University.

Figure 3.3: Projected sprawl for Atlanta, Georgia, Alabama, and North Carolina Economic Area: (a) uncontrolled growth scenario; (b) controlled growth scenario.

could escape sprawl. Under the sprawling scenario, sprawl counties would each become home to an average of almost 15,000 new households, while the more urban counties would take on an average of 68,000 new residents. If growth were redirected, the average growth of households in sprawling counties would drop to about 8,100, while in six counties designated for growth it would increase by an average

(a)

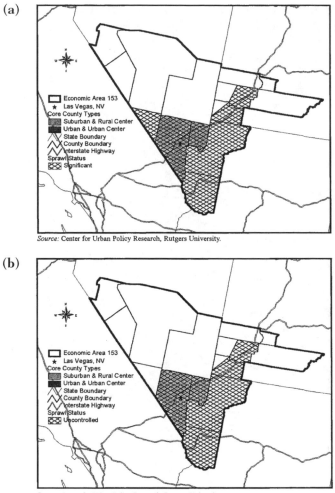

Source: Center for Urban Policy Research, Rutgers University.

(b)

Source: Center for Urban Policy Research, Rutgers University.

FIGURE 3.4: Projected sprawl for Las Vegas, Nevada, Arizona, and Utah Economic Area: (a) uncontrolled growth scenario; (b) controlled growth scenario.

of more than 90,000 households. Bartow and Hall counties are projected to continue to sprawl because neighboring counties would not have the capacity to absorb their growth.

LAS VEGAS

An example of a region where an urban growth boundary would probably have little impact in controlling sprawl, Las Vegas is growing rapidly with a very limited urban core. The area's eleven large counties are divided between sprawling counties and slow-growth rural areas; for this survey, the large counties are subdivided into sections. Clark County, in which the city of Las Vegas is located, is so large, so spread out, and of such low density that every section is considered a sprawling suburban location. As a result, no counties or sections with urban densities are available to absorb the region's considerable growth. For this reason, under the Rutgers analysis, sprawl in Las Vegas is not controlled (Figure 3.4). This is not to say that smart growth techniques could not aid Las Vegas's considerable challenges in traffic, water, and other areas, but that—for our analysis—redirection of development is unlikely to control sprawl.

Conclusion

Sprawl can best be contained in regions with moderate growth and center city areas that are reasonably viable yet in need of economic redevelopment. In other, high-growth areas with growing central cities in counties where significant land remains, redirecting outer-county sprawl may cause inner counties to sprawl at a higher density. Even though outer areas would be protected, inner areas may experience heightened sprawl. Sprawl, defined as low-density, leapfrog development beyond existing cities and towns, cannot be controlled as effectively through urban growth boundaries in very high growth areas. These two development scenarios give us the base to look more closely at the price that government, individuals, and businesses may end up paying for continued sprawl development well into the twenty-first century.

Chapter 4

Watash Mountain Range, Salt Lake City, Utah. Photograph by Catherine Galley.

Land and Natural Resource Consequences of Sprawl

SPRAWL CONSUMES LAND. From 1982 to 1997, the U.S. population grew by 17 percent while urbanized land grew by 47 percent.[1] Between 1970 and 1990, the Chicago metropolitan area grew by 46 percent while its population increased by only 4 percent. The Cleveland urban area expanded by 33 percent in that same period while its regional population declined by 11 percent. This inefficient use of land is part of the reason that farmland, natural areas, and other open space seem to be disappearing quickly, particularly close to urban areas. An estimated 2.2 million acres of prime farmland, forests, wetlands, and other open space are converted into developed land each year.[2]

Over the period 2000 to 2025, under traditional sprawling development, the United States is expected to lose about 7 million acres of farmland and 7 million acres of environmentally fragile lands to real estate development. Another 5 million acres of other lands, mostly smaller, barren plots, will also be lost. In total, 18.8 million acres of farmland and other open space will be lost to development. During this period, developers are expected to build 26.5 million housing units and 26.5 billion square feet of nonresidential space. Land would be converted at a rate of approximately 0.6 acre per residential unit and 0.2 acre per 1,000 square feet of nonresidential space.

Consensus exists nationally that air and water in the United States should be free from pollution. However, despite the obvious benefits, there is no similar broad-based agreement that lands should be protected from development. In fact, the reverse is true. Each citizen has a constitutional right to own land free from governmental interference, and governments must be careful to avoid land use regulations that could be interpreted as a taking of private property. Certain public policies, such as the development of the interstate highway system, further encourage access to land at the periphery of metropolitan areas. Such policies render land vulnerable to development, land that often is not lying fallow but is in agricultural production or is providing valuable natural habitat. The loss of these lands is a cost of sprawl.

But some would argue that not all is lost, that we are merely replacing some public open space with personal open space and providing more opportunities to set aside public open space closer to residential areas.

Can Sprawl Provide Open Space?

Historically, personal open space has been highly desired by most Americans. In surveys conducted by the Federal National Mortgage Agency, prospective home buyers want not only yards but yards on all sides. Sprawl's development of outlying green space provides larger and more accessible open space in the form of private yards, which can provide aesthetic and recreational benefits to the public without the use of taxpayers' funds. Some would argue that large, unsettled sites "inboard" of the subdivision farthest from the urban core can eventually be set aside for inner-suburban or urban open space as this becomes a local priority.

However, except in the wealthiest and most resilient of inner suburbs, open space is almost never a choice or option of local government. Most governments in these localities are pressed for fiscal resources and dispose of these land parcels to the highest bidder. The abutting properties, rather than receiving permanently improved open space, are often subject to more intensive and occasionally disruptive land uses, such as office park development, which can pay more in taxes. Thus, although a potential for inner-city/suburban open space appears to be the result of skipped-over lands, rarely does new open space materialize in either developed or redeveloping neighborhoods.

The setting aside of open space for public use by residents of an entire region may also be "underfinanced" in sprawl-dominated areas compared to those with more regionally oriented governance structures. Motivated by fiscal pressures to provide benefits for only their own residents, municipal governments may be unwilling to devote resources to creating facilities for use by persons throughout a region.

Farmland

Farmland is a finite natural resource threatened by sprawl. The American Farmland Trust reports that 86 percent of fruits and vegetables and 63 percent of dairy products produced in the United States come from urban-influenced areas. Between 1982 and 1992, Michigan lost 854,000 acres of farmland—about 10 acres every hour—to new development. Similar statistics describe growth patterns all across the country.

Farms, ranches, and the rest of the food production system in the United States contribute nearly $1 trillion annually to the national economy—about 13 percent of the gross national product. The United States is a major exporter of food products.[3] In addition to the obvious benefits of food production, crops and farmland offer habitat to birds, other wildlife, and a host of insects and small creatures that perform such functions as pollination and decomposition. Farmlands, when worked responsibly, filter pollutants from the water and air and even play a role in moderating the absorption of rains and preventing floods. Agriculture also generates secondary benefits that are enjoyed by rural and nonrural residents alike, including rural and pastoral scenery, recreational facilities, environmental quality, wildlife habitats, air and water recharge areas, fresh-quality food products, and greenery.

Other issues involving the loss of agricultural land to sprawl do not constitute physical loss but do involve loss of function. The difficulty of conducting efficient farming operations near residential subdivisions reduces the productivity of that land. Subdividing land into small lots for residential purposes inhibits farmers' ability to operate on large contiguous land parcels, thereby reducing the efficiency of mechanized agricultural operations. Further, under sprawl development, subdivisions and farms may be interspersed, causing some residents to object to the odors, noise, truck traffic, and other local conditions associated with active agricultural uses. When such contiguous development occurs, local governments sometimes opt to impose restrictions on farming.

These difficult farming conditions bring about an "impermanence syndrome" that is antithetical to sustained farmland productivity. In rural areas that can be readily developed, high land values often shift farmers' profit motive from agricultural operations to capital gains from real estate sales. The real estate sales, in turn, reduce the average farm size, thus limiting the realization of economies of scale—a characteristic of U.S. agriculture. Various other restraints on farmland productivity—ranging from restrictive regulations to recurring vandalism—have also been imposed. All of these factors mean farmers may hesitate to invest in new technology and farm infrastructure due to impending development. Land remains idle, awaiting conversion to other uses. Studies involving sprawl development allege that this impermanence syndrome reduces farmland productivity.

Growth through sprawl also expands demand for water for urban uses and thereby reduces the amount of water available for agriculture. Agriculture currently uses much more water than urban settlements in many states where farming depends on irrigation, such as

Arizona, California, Colorado, Oklahoma, and Texas. As urban settlements expand in these areas, more water will have to be diverted
from agriculture to supply the basic needs of the resident population.
This diversion will restrict the operation of farming in such areas.
Single-family property owners and corporate commercial facilities
also often use vast amounts of water for lawn sprinkling, an excessive use of this natural resource needed for food production.

The environmental and social benefits of agriculture are public
goods. By definition, public goods are those goods that everyone
wants but few are willing to produce because the market does not
provide a compensatory mechanism for producers. Economists refer
to this phenomenon as market failure. To ensure the production of
public goods, the government usually intervenes by supporting such
production with taxes levied on all of society. In the case of agriculture, however, the public benefits—fresh air, open space, recreational facilities, and so on—are produced free of charge to the public. U.S. farmers are not compensated for these goods, despite their
importance to society. When farmers sell their lands, these benefits
are lost.

Environmentally Fragile Lands

Open space, such as forests, meadows, and wetlands, also provides
valuable benefits—and is also at high risk. Each year between 1997
and 2001, more than a million acres of forestland were converted to
developed uses. The analysis here focuses on environmentally fragile lands, areas that are particularly vulnerable to the activities of
nature and human beings. These types of lands do not lend themselves well to development. The primary types of water-based, environmentally fragile lands are floodplains, wetlands, and critical sensitive watersheds; the geologically based fragile lands include steep
slopes, sinkholes, and erosion-prone lands.

The effects of disturbing aquifers, streams, and wetlands can
range from flooding to drought to poor water quality. Wetlands work
as natural sponges, soaking up and storing rain and runoff while also

FIGURE 4.1: Wetlands, eastern Pennsylvania subdivision. Photograph by George Lowenstein.

cleaning stormwater of pollutants—a cost-effective way of improving water quality and managing stormwater. Sprawling development can destroy or impair wetlands, increasing the amount of polluted runoff flowing into rivers and lakes and increasing the risk of flooding.

Each year, development disrupts wildlife habitat by claiming millions of acres of wetlands and forests. This loss often results in habitat fragmentation, in which animals are forced to live in smaller areas isolated from other members of their own species and sometimes unable to forage or migrate effectively. Habitat destruction is the main factor threatening 80 percent or more of the species listed under the Endangered Species Act.[4] Open space also provides valuable recreational opportunities and benefits too numerous to evaluate here.

In some areas, the economic value of wetlands and other open space has been calculated in terms of how they can save the costs of human-made infrastructure that serves the same purpose. For example, the New York City Watershed Agreement, which helped purchase eighty thousand acres within the watershed providing New

York City's drinking water, provides an enhanced watershed protection program. Although the multiyear agreement is costing $1.4 billion to implement, the plan allows New York City to avoid the construction of filtration facilities estimated to cost between $6 billion and $8 billion.[5]

It is clear that the personal open space provided in sprawling areas through yards with lawns does not provide the extensive benefits gained by preserving farmland, pastureland, forests, wetlands, and other undeveloped areas.

Controlling Sprawl to Save Land

Controlling sprawl is in many ways fundamentally about saving land, and the growth-control measures we used in our analysis show significant savings. With both types of growth-control measures in place, 4 million acres, or almost a quarter of the 19 million acres expected to be converted under sprawl, could be maintained as open space without compromising growth or altering housing markets (Table 4.1). The first measure employs the equivalent of an urban growth boundary in metropolitan areas to direct growth to the more developed urban and suburban counties and away from rural and undeveloped counties; 2.4 million acres could be saved through this redirection. The second measure uses an equivalent of an urban service area in individual counties to focus development in already built up areas in the same county; an additional 1.6 million acres could be saved through this redirection.

Included in the above land savings are approximately 1.5 million acres of agricultural land, 1.5 million acres of environmentally fragile land, and 1.0 million acres of other lands (e.g., barren). The South and the West, where sprawl is most extensive, could save 2.14 million acres and 1.14 million acres (21.5 percent and almost 25 percent), respectively. Smaller land savings take place in the Northeast and Midwest regions, which would save 19 percent and 16 percent, respectively.

In looking at land conversion in metropolitan regions as defined

TABLE 4.1
Land Saved under Compact Growth Scenario, United States, 2000–2025
(in Acres)

Agricultural Lands	Environmentally Fragile Lands	Other Lands	Total Land
1,499,636	1,505,434	997,156	4,002,231

Source: Center for Urban Policy Research, Rutgers University.

by Economic Areas, the place expected to lose the most open space to sprawling development is Atlanta. Sprawling development is expected to convert 800,000 acres of open space to development, a conversion of more than half an acre per development unit. Controlling Atlanta's growth with growth boundaries and service areas would be expected to save more than 245,000 acres, or 30 percent. The Washington, DC–Baltimore region would save the highest percentage of threatened lands, saving almost 40 percent (265,000 acres) of lands that are projected to be lost to sprawl.

The analysis above shows that noticeable land savings can be achieved by redirecting growth. Urban growth boundaries that redirect growth to more developed counties account for 60 percent of the savings, while urban service areas that focus growth within a county account for 40 percent of the savings. These methods of controlling sprawl could produce a 4-million-acre projected land savings nationwide over the next twenty-five years without obviously affecting real property markets. While this acreage savings is significant, it still is only 0.3 percent of all nonfederal rural land. Further, the agricultural land savings (1.5 million acres) is only 0.5 percent of the cropland and pastures we are now using.

Separate studies in several states and regions have found similar results, notably in New Jersey, Lexington, Kentucky, the Delaware Estuary, Michigan, South Carolina, and the San Francisco Bay area. These analyses employed land conversion models to compare sprawl development scenarios and more compact approaches.

The studies used different densities, different development locations, and, occasionally, different housing types under the alternatives for future growth, but all found significant savings in the

TABLE 4.2
Land Conversion Savings of Compact Growth

Area of Impact	Lexington, KY, and Delaware Estuary	Michigan	South Carolina	New Jersey	California
Land/Natural habitat preservation					
Developable land	20.5–24.2%	15.5%	15%	6%	55%
Agricultural land	18–29%	17.4%	18%	39%	50%
Environmentally fragile land	20–27%	20.9%	22%	17%	100%

Sources: Burchell (1992–1997); Landis (1995).

amount of land that would be converted (Table 4.2). The studies of Lexington and the Delaware Estuary showed projected twenty- to twenty-five-year savings in the conversion of agricultural and environmentally fragile acreage of roughly 20 to 30 percent under compact versus sprawl development. Michigan and South Carolina would be expected to save about 20 percent each; New Jersey could save 40 percent of projected agricultural losses and 20 percent of environmentally fragile lands. The results in the San Francisco Bay area were even more pronounced. The most compact types of development saved nearly 50 percent of farmland acreage and steep-sloped areas, and close to 100 percent of wetland areas. The latter are components of environmentally fragile lands.

Sustaining agriculture is one of the more efficient ways to guarantee production of the public goods and amenities provided by open space. First, much of the undeveloped land in the United States is currently in agriculture. Second, agriculture can allow open space retention through private ownership of land, so that government does not have to purchase farms outright in order to preserve open space. Third, of all the ways known to retain open space, agriculture makes the most productive use of land. It allows continued production, employment, and value added. Fourth, agriculture maintains the flexibility of future land use, as it involves little transformation of land from its natural form.

Ample developable land exists to accommodate projected population growth in developing and developed areas of the United States without unduly harming environmentally sensitive lands. With careful planning, accommodating growth and accommodating environmental protection need not be mutually exclusive goals. "Reasonable" compact growth policies could significantly reduce the amount of undeveloped land needed to accommodate projected population growth in the United States. Such policies would neither seek to substitute urban for suburban living nor promote significantly higher density in existing urban areas. Instead, they would advocate small increases in rural and developing-suburban residential densities while also encouraging urban and inner-suburban communities to create new infill opportunities.

Chapter 5

Construction of the Marsha Sharp Freeway, Lubbock, Texas. Photograph by Catherine Galley.

Infrastructure Consequences

THE COST OF SPRAWL that may be easiest to measure and easiest to grasp is that of infrastructure: the miles of extra pipe and extra asphalt that it takes to reach spread-out homes, offices, and schools with water, sewer lines, and roads. This chapter compares the costs of sprawling versus compact growth, beginning with water and sewer infrastructure and concluding with road infrastructure. Providing this infrastructure can burden local governments, which in turn can lead to higher taxes. In Chapter 7, we'll discuss the costs of providing other community services, such as schools, and the overall fiscal impact this may have on local governments.

Sprawl increases infrastructure costs in several ways. Lower density means each yard of linear infrastructure—water and sewer mains, roadways, even curbs—serves fewer households. More compact development would allow the same amount of infrastructure to serve more households.

The segregation of land uses associated with sprawl raises costs even further because parallel infrastructure systems often have to be provided to individual residential and nonresidential locations. In addition, sprawl's leapfrog development, which locates growth away from existing development, does not capitalize on pockets of surplus infrastructure capacity that may already be present in and around existing development. Finally, fragmented governance, a seemingly natural accompaniment to sprawl, often leads to duplicative water and sewer treatment facilities, and even to duplicative city halls, police stations, courts, firehouses, and schools.

These costs were documented back in the original *Costs of Sprawl* study in 1974 (discussed in Chapter 1) and have been confirmed in several studies since. One real-world case study of some communities in Florida found that providing utilities had cost almost 40 percent more per dwelling unit under sprawl than under several forms of compact development; roads had cost 60 percent more per dwelling unit.[1] Looking at development over the next twenty-five years, how might differing development patterns affect how much governments and citizens spend to provide water, sewer, and roads?

Water and Sewer

Water and sewer costs arise from three factors: the demand for water and sewer services, the number of hookups to water mains, and the type of water system used. All of these factors are influenced by the way a community develops and the types of houses that are built.

DEMAND

The national average for water consumption per capita in 1999 was 112 gallons per day. Business and industrial use ranges from 5 percent to 20 percent of this number. With a projected population growth of more than 60.7 million, nationwide residential and nonresidential growth during the period 2000 to 2025 will require additional local water and sewer capacity to provide more than 9 billion gallons of water and the treatment of more than 8 billion gallons of sewage.

The amount of water-based utility infrastructure needed is directly related to demand for water and for sewage treatment; the type of development has a direct impact on this demand. Single-family detached homes use more water, simply because people water their lawns. High-end office parks with expanses of land also tend to water more lawn. In a study comparing development forms in New

Jersey during the 1990s, lawn watering was found to be the primary reason for differences in water demand.[2] Sewer demand (sanitary sewers only, not storm sewers) parallels water demand but is lower because not all of the water remains in the system for disposal. The quantity remaining varies from 80 percent to 97 percent of the total water consumption for residential and nonresidential uses—and septic systems do not return any of the water for treatment.

For the two growth scenarios, we calculated that a single-family detached home with a slightly larger than average household size (2.86 persons) consumes 431 gallons of water per day and that 257 gallons of that water returns to the system and needs sewage treatment. Sixty-four gallons is used to water lawns and plants. Water and sewer demand is less for other types of housing, mainly because of reduced outdoor water consumption.

Nonresidential uses are harder to standardize, but for this analysis, each one thousand square feet of nonresidential space is defined as a single unit, and standard numbers are assumed for employees per square feet for office, retail, industrial, and warehouse uses. Water consumption is calculated at approximately 35 to 40 gallons per day per employee. For industrial uses, product use and internal cleaning increase water consumption per employee by one-third. For all nonresidential uses, outdoor water use is 2 percent to 3 percent of the total water demand.

As discussed in Chapter 3, both the sprawling and the compact development scenarios project that the United States will need 26.5 million new homes and 26.5 million new units of commercial, retail, and institutional space over the twenty-five-year period from 2000 to 2025. In the sprawl development scenario, of the 53 million development units, 33.6 million will be in urban and suburban counties and 19.4 million will be in rural and undeveloped counties. The United States would need to add an average of 106.5 gallons of water and 90.0 gallons of sewage capacity per day per person. Of the four main census regions of the United States, the South will require the largest portion of new water and sewer infrastructure (44 percent of the nationwide total), because it will experience the greatest amount of growth over the next twenty-five years. In 2025, the South will require an additional 4.2 billion gallons of domestic water and an additional 3.7 billion gallons of sewer capacity daily. The West, which will experience the second-largest growth of the census regions, will require an additional daily capacity of 3.1 billion and 2.7 billion gallons of water and sewer, respectively. The Midwest will require an additional 2.9 billion gallons of water per day, and 1.4 billion gallons of sewer capacity. This is twice the level of the Northeast, at 0.77 billion and 0.68 billion gallons of additional water and sewer capacity, respectively.

Under the compact growth scenario, 3.1 million development units (homes, offices, and so forth) would be shifted within the region to the more urban and suburban counties, a shift of more than 9.2 percent. Within the counties, another 2 million units would be relocated to already-developed areas. These shifts would reduce the requirements for additional water capacity by almost 149 million gallons per day and sewer capacity by 7 million gallons per day. This is a 1.5 percent savings in water and sewer capacity during the period 2000 to 2025, due almost exclusively to the projected 25 percent decrease in the number of single-family detached homes with large lawns that need water. Nonresidential demand would remain essentially the same because of the low rate of lawn watering for these types of uses and the very little change in types of units under the two scenarios.

The largest percentage reduction in water demand occurs in the West, which would save 1.8 percent, or 54 million gallons per day. The South would save the most in absolute terms, consuming 68 million fewer gallons, a savings of 1.6 percent; sewage needs would drop by 4.1 million gallons, or 0.1 percent. The smallest savings in additional capacity would occur in the Northeast and the Midwest for water, with savings of 8.9 million and 17.9 million gallons per day, respectively. The Northeast would actually experience a modest increase in sewer demand of 1.9 million gallons per day.

Other factors related to growth may also affect water demand and savings. For example, opponents of sprawl are paying increasing attention to its impact on overall water quality and hydrology. Sprawl-ing development creates more impervious surface area, which leads to faster runoff of stormwater into streams and rivers, preventing the recharge of groundwater systems and reducing residential and municipal water supplies.[3] This loss can be reversed through growth that reduces impervious surfaces and through low-impact develop-ment techniques that capture water on-site.

WATER AND SEWER HOOKUPS: LATERALS

While demand is only slightly lower in a smart growth future, the cost of supplying water-related infrastructure is significantly less. These costs include treatment plants, storage tanks, distribution and collection mains, and—perhaps most significantly—the hookups between individual buildings and the mains. These small pipes are referred to as *laterals*.

During the period 2000 to 2025, if sprawling growth continues unabated, developers and local governments in the United States will have to put into the ground nearly 46 million water and sewer laterals to service new residential and nonresidential structures. With compact growth measures in place, a new housing pattern would mean fewer water and sewer laterals would be needed to serve an equivalent number of homes, commercial establishments, and offices. The 46 million new water and sewer laterals under the sprawl growth scenario would be reduced to 41.2 million new water and sewer laterals under the compact growth scenario, a savings of 4.6 million laterals, or about 10 percent (Table 5.1).

The main source of this savings in hookups is the shift from single-family houses, which each require their own lateral, to attached townhomes and multifamily condominiums and apart-ments that share a single lateral. Under the smart growth scenario, there would be about 25 percent more of these types of homes. In addition, the portion of single-family homes using wells and septic systems would drop. The decrease in these types of homes means the number of wells and septic systems serving single-family homes —each counted as one lateral—would drop from 13.8 million to 11.4

TABLE 5.1
Savings in Water and Sewer Infrastructure under
Compact Growth Scenario, United States, 2000–2025

	Number of New Water and Sewer Laterals	Cost of New Water and Sewer Infrastructure
Sprawl growth scenario	45,866,594	$189,767,000,000
Compact growth scenario	41,245,294	$177,160,000,000
Savings	4,621,303	$12,609,000,000
Percent savings	10.1	6.6

Source: Center for Urban Policy Research, Rutgers University.

million. All of the reduction in laterals comes from these housing changes. Nonresidential buildings are mostly projected to be of the same size in the two scenarios and would not experience a significant change in the number of laterals needed.

The region with the largest overall future demand, the South, would generally require the largest number of new water and sewer laterals and would also experience the largest absolute reduction in laterals under compact growth—a savings of 2.1 million laterals, or a 10 percent reduction. The West would experience the largest percentage reduction, needing 11.7 percent fewer laterals (1.7 million laterals). The Northeast region would have the smallest absolute reduction in laterals, 0.3 million (a 9.9 percent reduction), while the Midwest would have the smallest percentage reduction of laterals, at 7.1 percent (0.5 million laterals).

Costs

In addition to the differing number of hookups for different types of homes, water systems vary by where development occurs, which affects water costs. Urban areas generally use water hookups from public systems, with some expansion into adjacent areas of urban counties and to the developed areas of suburban counties. The undeveloped areas of suburban counties generally use package water treatment facilities, which are off-the-shelf units that provide communities with chemical feeders, sedimentation basins, filters, and other elements of the treatment process in a prefabricated assembly.

This is also the case for developed areas of rural and undeveloped counties. Water and sewer service in undeveloped areas of rural and undeveloped counties is provided by individually dug or drilled wells and septic tanks.

Users of water and sewer services generally pay a hookup or tap-in fee that covers their share of the entire water system, whatever its type. The tap-in fee and the shared cost of a unit's lateral make up the cost of connecting to water and sewer systems.

For single-family homes in an undeveloped part of suburbia using a package system, the typical tap-in fee to the public system is $2,000 and the typical sewer tap-in fee is $4,300. The cost of the lateral is $1,200 for water and $1,000 for sewer; the total cost of providing water and sewer infrastructure is $8,500. The tap-in fees for a single-family home in an urban area typically totals $6,540, with costs of $1,310 for water and $2,813 for sewer, and with water and sewer lateral costs of $1,320 and $1,100, respectively. Homes in developed parts of suburbia cost $7,000 to service as part of a public water and sewer system. Individual wells and septic systems used in homes in rural areas cost about $9,600 apiece. Attached single-family homes and multifamily buildings have lower per-unit costs: water and sewer service for a townhouse in an undeveloped suburban area costs about $6,755, while service for a townhouse in the city costs about $5,050 (Table 5.2).

For our analysis, urban county costs also reflect the increased replacement costs of a county's aging infrastructure. The cost of the individual on-site wells or septic systems includes the costs of pumping and transfer equipment. Typical installation costs of water and sewer laterals are 10 percent higher in suburban versus rural counties and 20 percent higher in urban as opposed to suburban counties, due to the difficulty of working in higher-density areas. The cost of the water laterals includes individual or shared meters. In addition, the typical costs are adjusted in each county to account for differences in labor costs.

Under a traditional, sprawling development pattern, total water and sewer infrastructure costs would be close to $190 billion, with

TABLE 5.2
Water/Sewer Infrastructure Costs by Type and Location of Unit

Type	Single-Family Detached	Single-Family Attached	Multifamily
Rural: septic	$9,600	n/a	n/a
Suburban: package	$8,500	$5,755	n/a
Urban: public system	$6,540	$5,050	$3,860

Source: Center for Urban Policy Research, Rutgers University.

water making up 40 percent of the combined cost. If, instead, the United States pursued the compact growth scenario and shifted about 5 million homes to more compact areas, with an increase in the number of attached and multifamily dwellings, the total cost for water and sewer infrastructure would drop to $177.2 billion. This $12.6 billion in savings—mainly a result of combined cost savings of lower tap-in fees and 4.6 million fewer laterals for infrastructure— amounts to a savings of about 7 percent. A part of that savings comes from the projected clustering of 20 percent of the single-family dwellings located in the outer portions of rural and undeveloped counties. In these clustered developments, package water and sewer systems replace wells and septic fields. The costs for these community systems are about $1,320 less per unit than septic systems.

The South would save the most by moving to a smart growth development pattern. The water and sewer infrastructure savings in the South, at $5.5 billion, equal one-half the projected savings nationwide. In the West, a $4.2 billion reduction in infrastructure costs would amount to a savings of 7.2 percent. The infrastructure savings in the Northeast and Midwest regions total $2.8 billion, 7.9 percent in the Northeast and only 5.1 percent in the Midwest. In all regions, sewer cost savings are 1.8 times those observed for water costs.

THE LOS ANGELES REGION

The greater Los Angeles region will require more water and sewer capacity over the next twenty-five years than any other metropolitan region in the nation. If growth continues uncontrolled, the region will require more than 500 million gallons each of daily water and sewer capacity—and about 2 million new water and sewer laterals. No other region even comes close to that level of need. The region also stands to save more than other regions if it turns to smarter growth patterns. The region would save 15.4 million gallons in water capacity each day and could avoid installing 477,000 new water and sewer laterals. These changes mean the region could save $1.26 billion in water and sewer infrastructure—a savings of more than 13 percent— by redirecting some development to more developed areas.

At the county level, the redirection of growth within the urban area means some suburban counties could experience dramatic reductions in their water and sewer burden, while more urban counties may actually experience an increase in demand. Between them, Riverside and San Bernardino counties would save 220 million gallons of future water and sewer need per day. Los Angeles County, on the other hand, would need to supply an additional 252 million gallons per day.

Summary

The potential savings in water and sewer infrastructure, laterals, and cost between the sprawl and compact growth scenarios are related primarily to differences in the number of laterals serving the more intense uses under the latter scenario. The number of laterals required is related to housing type. The dispersion and spatial relationship of housing units (characterized by type) determine the length and complexity of water and sewer distribution and collection mains, which translate directly to cost. Housing type and location affect the number of water and sewer laterals and resultant costs.

Road Infrastructure

Another major infrastructure system affected by development patterns is the road network. As mentioned in Chapter 1, past studies looking at road infrastructure costs have found that sprawling places need—and build—more miles of roadway. In particular, the long-

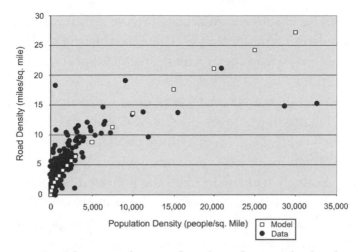

FIGURE 5.1: Road density as a function of population density in developed areas of all counties in the study.

running study of infrastructure costs for the state of New Jersey found that in sprawling locations when more land was consumed for development, more lane-miles were needed for state and local roads. Road costs for sprawling development were found to be as much as 25 percent higher than in compact places.

Many factors influence the demand for roads, and transportation engineers have developed elaborate four-step models to predict that demand. Transportation researchers have determined that land use has an impact on how much people travel by car, which also influences the need for roads. More compact places, with more destinations accessible by foot, bicycle, or transit, generate fewer automobile trips. Fundamentally important in comparing the relative benefits and costs of different growth patterns, this issue is also referred to in Chapters 7, 8, and 9.

The analysis in this current chapter is primarily concerned with infrastructure costs, so instead of using complex demand modeling, it projects future road demand based on population density and urban form. The advantage of this approach is the very strong historical correlation between population density and the density of road miles in a given area, which shows that population density is a good predictor of future road density (Figure 5.1). It also uses data readily available for most counties (lane-miles of local roads) and for every state (cost of road construction), an important consideration in a national study.

The model determines the future need for roads based on the historical relationship between population density and the density of the road network; it assumes that future development will be served by a similar pattern of local roads and projects local road requirements accordingly. The model takes the projected population density in 2025 and determines an ideal road density for each developed and undeveloped area of each county. The need for new road construction is predicted by comparing this ideal level of required lane-miles with the existing lane-miles found in a county. If an area does not have enough roads to match the projected future density, the extra road infrastructure and its costs were added to the model. In some cases, the county's existing capacity may be enough to accommodate future growth; in these cases, no new miles of roadway were added.

Using this model, sprawling growth is expected to require more than 2 million additional collector and local road lane-miles by 2025. These additional lane-miles will be in the form of either new roads or supplemental lanes added to existing roads. Developed areas will need only 174,000 lane-miles, less than one-tenth the need in undeveloped areas, where 1.97 million lane-miles will need to be built. This is because the undeveloped areas that do not have an extensive road infrastructure in place yet would receive the bulk of growth under the sprawl growth scenario.

The cost to construct these required lane-miles in the United States during the period 2000 to 2025 would be $927 billion in 2000 dollars (Table 5.3). These costs can be attributed solely to the construction of the new lane-miles of roads, excluding both required structures and land acquisition.

Under the compact or smart growth scenario, the additional lane-miles of local roads needed would be reduced by 188,000 lane-miles, a decrease of more than 9 percent nationwide. The West

TABLE 5.3
Savings in Road Construction under Compact
Growth Scenario, United States, 2000–2025

	Miles of New Roads	Cost of New Roads
Sprawl growth scenario	2,044,179	$927,010,000,000
Compact growth scenario	1,855,874	$817,310,000,000
Savings	188,305	$109,700,000,000

Source: Center for Urban Policy Research, Rutgers University.

would save the most through a compact growth scenario, as it could avoid building 85,000 lane-miles. This is more than 45 percent of all lane-miles saved nationwide. The West would realize these savings because it is expected to grow significantly and has started with a less dense network of roads in relation to its population density. The South would save 79,000 lane-miles, and the Midwest would save 17,500 lane-miles. The Northeast shows the least number of lane-miles saved, at 7,000. This is because it has less growth and an existing road network that is already quite extensive.

In calculating road costs, the model takes into account development standards for roads (lane widths, center dividers, sidewalks, and so forth) that affect the costs of roadway construction. These standards are typically different for rural roads, where a two-lane highway with five-foot-wide shoulders may be sufficient, than they are for urban roads, where the standards may include curbs, gutters, and a twelve-foot auxiliary lane.

Both national and state sources provide per-mile construction costs for urban and rural development environments. One lane-mile of rural road in an undeveloped area is projected to cost $500,000, suburban roads in developed areas cost an estimated $1 million per mile, and urban roads cost $1.2 million per mile. These typical costs have been adjusted to account for different labor costs in individual counties. For consistency, the study used concrete roadway construction costs. Asphalt-surfaced roads typically cost 20 to 25 percent less than concrete. Most new roads, especially in the Southeast, Southwest, and West regions of the United States, are concrete. While new lanes can be added by widening existing roadways, the cost of widening roadways is only 10 to 20 percent less per lane-mile than new construction when land acquisition costs are not included.

The need to build fewer roads under the smart growth scenario results in significant cost savings. The total cost for added road infrastructure under the compact scenario is just over $817 billion, compared with the $927 billion that would be spent under the sprawl growth scenario (see Table 5.3). This is a savings of $110 billion, or almost 12 percent. The savings in the West is by far the largest dollar value—$56 billion, or 51 percent of the total. The road lane-mile cost savings in the West equals the total lane-mile cost savings in the rest of the country. In the South, road infrastructure costs would be reduced by $39 billion; the local road lane-mile infrastructure savings in the Midwest and the Northeast are projected to be about $8.6 billion and $6.2 billion, respectively.

In looking at road cost savings by regions, two California metropolitan regions stand to save the most by shifting growth toward already-developed areas. The greater Los Angeles region and the San Francisco Bay area would save 18,375 lane-miles and 9,602 lane-miles, respectively. Los Angeles would save $15.9 billion, while San Francisco would save at least $8.25 billion. Among counties, two jurisdictions in the Los Angeles region would also save the most: Los Angeles County would save 6,500 lane-miles and $8 billion, while Riverside County would avoid building 4,700 lane-miles at a cost of $2.33 billion.

These savings are most likely conservative. The model is based entirely on the cost of building the road itself and does not take into account the cost of land acquisition or of bridges, both significant elements of road construction. Only collectors and local roads are used in this model, leaving out national (for example, interstates) and state highways, which are less affected by local development patterns. Since the input used in the road-demand function is total length of roads, not the number of lanes, an average roadway width of two lanes was assumed. The model also looks only at the cost of building new roads, not at the cost of repairing and maintaining an ever-expanding road network.

Summary and Conclusion

The cost of required future water/sewer and road infrastructure in the United States under a sprawling growth scenario comes to slightly more than $21,000 per residential and nonresidential development unit, or a total of $1.12 trillion over a twenty-five-year period. Compact growth patterns would reduce this combined infrastructure cost to $18,750 per unit. The infrastructure savings due to compact growth would be $126 billion, or almost 11 percent. This is a particularly significant savings because these funds come primarily from local (municipal and county) budgets. The savings could allow local governments to spend more on infrastructure system preservation, which is in dire need of this funding. The finding is also significant because local politicians are reluctant to raise this type of money by imposing new forms of taxes and charges. Chapter 7 will discuss the fiscal impact of providing this infrastructure and other community services.

Dually supporting and underutilizing two systems of infrastructure—one that is being abandoned in and around central cities and close-in suburbs, and one that is not yet fully used in rural areas just beginning to be developed—is causing governments to forgo the maintenance of much infrastructure and the provision of anything *other* than growth-related infrastructure. The United States, in other words, is funding road infrastructure by:

- not funding all infrastructure
- not *fully* funding developmental infrastructure
- not repairing or replacing most types of infrastructure
- not taking advantage of technological improvements in the rehabilitation, repair, and provision of infrastructure that could be passed on to taxpayers as savings.

Chapter 6

Hiram Square, downtown New Brunswick, New Jersey. Photograph by Catherine Galley.

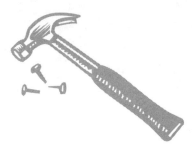

Real Estate Development Costs

WHAT WILL IT COST to build all the homes, offices, and other buildings required to house the population and employment growth expected during the next twenty-five years? Would more compact development lower these costs? When implementing growth management, development should take place in more central locations, saving land at the periphery. This should be accomplished without raising property development costs. If the processes that are used to contain development are too growth limited or intrusive, they may well increase the costs of residential and nonresidential development. This has been one of the prime arguments made against urban growth boundaries in Oregon and elsewhere.[1]

It does seem to make sense that restricting the supply of land available for housing would increase housing costs. However, the cost of housing is complex and is influenced by many factors, including location, the variety of housing being built, demand, and mobility options. Typically, in urban center, urban, suburban, and rural center counties, densities are higher and buildings have higher floor-area ratios (FARS), the ratio of the floor area of the building to the size of its lot. This often lowers the per unit land cost of property development as well as the prices of the properties developed. In rural and undeveloped counties, densities and FARS are lower, which raises the

land component of property costs and the prices of developed properties in typically higher-priced locations. The greater variety of
housing types available under a compact growth scenario also means
lower overall housing costs, because more lower-cost attached and
multifamily housing is available.

To determine the effects of sprawl and compact growth development futures on housing costs, our study calculated the prices of various types of new housing for each of the counties using data from
the U.S. Census and the American Housing Survey. Price by structure type, including the value of multifamily units determined
through rent capitalization, was split into land and structure components: land costs are approximately 25 percent of total costs for
single-family detached dwellings, 20 percent for single-family
attached dwellings, 60 percent for mobile homes, and 10 percent for
multifamily dwellings. In determining the cost of constructing nonresidential property, a cost per square foot was determined for each
type of nonresidential property (office space, retail, industrial, and
warehouse) and adjusted to reflect different labor costs in different
counties.

Sprawl and Development Costs

To accommodate the growth of 23.5 million new households—and
the corresponding growth of 49.4 million new jobs—the sprawl
growth scenario requires the construction of residential and nonresidential space costing $6.4 trillion during the period 2000 to 2025.
Sixty-nine percent of this total, or $4.4 trillion, would be required for
residential development; 31 percent, or $2 trillion, would be required
for nonresidential development. Under the sprawl growth scenario,
the value of single-family detached development is one-third the cost
of all development.

The nationwide average residential development cost per unit in
2000 dollars would be $167,038 per home under the sprawl growth
scenario. Residential value represents the average cost for all households. It is a combination of all housing types, ranging from the

relatively high-cost single-family detached home to the relatively low-cost multifamily apartments or condominiums. Residential and nonresidential costs in the Midwest and the South are lower than the U.S. averages, while those in the Northeast and the West exceed the nationwide averages.

Compact Growth and Development Costs

A more compact growth scenario offers the potential to lower property development costs because higher density means per-unit land costs will be lower and a greater mix of housing types means more lower-cost units will be built.

Under the compact growth scenario, the density of all development types is expected to increase by 20 percent. A density increase of this amount can often be accommodated with good design; a visitor would not be able to tell that the development is of higher density than average. By keeping density changes to this level, differences would not be apparent to the uninformed eye. Further, the growth of single-family attached and multifamily housing types is expected to increase by 25 percent over the sprawl scenario. In the undeveloped areas of all counties, overall density is not expected to increase, but approximately 20 percent of the residential units are expected to be developed in cluster developments wherein density is twice as high as the prevailing density of undeveloped areas. Additionally, all residential units redirected into developed areas were priced 5 percent higher than sprawl growth units to accommodate the expected increased amenities in housing units demanded by these households.

The increase in density should result in lower per-unit land costs. For example, if a new single-family dwelling costs $160,000, then $120,000 is assumed to be structure cost and $40,000 the land cost. If density is increased by 10 percent under compact development, the land portion of overall housing costs is lower. In this example, land costs would decline to $36,000, for a total cost of $156,000. The difference in housing costs in urban areas versus more peripheral

FIGURE 6.1: Kentlands Center, Gaithersburg, Maryland. Photograph courtesy of Island Press.

locations is a function of the variety of housing types offered closer in, where housing options tend to be smaller and more densely situated with a higher proportion of rental properties.

Under the compact growth scenario, overall development costs are projected to be reduced by $420 billion (Table 6.1). This amounts to a decrease in costs of nearly 7 percent nationwide. Average property development costs under compact growth are lowered in every region. Under the compact growth scenario, the average cost of a home would be expected to be $154,035, which is 8 percent lower than under the sprawl scenario. Among the thirty largest metropolitan areas, the average price of homes is considerably higher, and the savings from compact growth are also greater: compact growth would save, on average, more than $16,000 per home in these areas, lowering the average cost from $192,132 to $175,725. A few regions, notably the San Diego Economic Area, could save as much as 15 percent on

TABLE 6.1
Property Development Savings under Compact Growth Scenario, United States, 2000–2025

	Per-Unit Property Development Costs ($)		Aggregate Property Development Costs ($ Billions)		
	Residential	Nonresidential	Residential	Nonresidential	Total
Sprawl growth scenario	167,038	75,463	4,377.3	1,998.1	6,375.4
Compact growth scenario	154,035	74,598	3,993.0	1,962.1	5,955.1
Savings	13,003	865	384.3	36.0	420.3
Percent savings	7.8	1.1	8.2	1.9	6.6

Source: Center for Urban Policy Research, Rutgers University.

housing costs by instituting such growth management measures as urban growth boundaries and urban service areas.

While some of these savings are due to increased density, they are in large part offset by increased expenses that come from building in a more developed area. In the end, the cost savings can be largely attributed to the increased number of more compact—hence smaller—attached townhouses, condominiums, and apartments.[2] Skeptics might argue that this would detract from home owners' and renters' quality of life. On the other hand, demographic and cultural shifts—such as the aging of the baby-boom generation—mean that more Americans will be looking for alternatives to single-family homes. More compact growth would better meet that demand. In addition, these centrally located townhouses, condominiums, and apartment homes are expected to offer lower transportation and energy costs and better access to jobs and a variety of urban amenities than do traditional suburban detached houses. Finally, the majority of housing built under the compact growth scenario would continue to be the traditional single-family home, ensuring that this housing option would not be in short supply.

Average nonresidential development cost savings per unit are less significant, with only a 1 percent savings nationwide under the compact growth scenario. Nonresidential construction changes are quite modest: density is expected to increase only in developed areas, while costs in undeveloped areas remain the same. The model assumes no change in the types of commercial, retail, and industrial space under the compact growth scenario. The redirection of businesses to more developed areas increases their construction costs, further eroding the savings achieved by the increased density.

Under compact growth, the South is expected to experience the largest overall savings of $170 billion, or approximately 7 percent of overall property development costs. The West would save, in aggregate, $144 billion, or more than 6 percent of overall property development costs. The Northeast would be expected to save $54 billion, or 8 percent of overall property development costs. The Midwest shows a similar amount saved—$52 billion, or 5 percent of overall property development costs. The Northeast and Midwest regions exhibit the least savings due to less growth and existing higher-density areas; the West and South regions exhibit the most savings due to their significant growth and lower overall population density.

Conclusion

One of the arguments often made against urban growth boundaries and other smart growth strategies is that their restrictions raise housing costs. Indeed, one of the stated benefits of sprawl is that the principle of "drive until you qualify" puts home ownership in reach of more people. However, such homes often lack certain amenities, such as nearby parks and access to public transit. Also, the supply of affordable housing is often restricted in these areas by exclusionary zoning practices that require large lots or that ban multifamily housing. The greater supply of less expensive attached and multi-family housing under compact growth means more people would be able to afford homes closer in, with access to public transit and other amenities.

If development costs are lower under a compact development scenario, why are the nation's builders not rushing to embrace compact growth? The long-term benefits of this type of development are obscured by several immediate considerations for developers and the banks that finance them. Compact growth is unfamiliar, and mixed-use elements are often seen by lenders as risky. Mixed-income developments may have an affordable housing component, which means subsidies, and such subsidies—whether from federal, state, or local sources—are complicated. Even the assembly of land may be complicated as developers must stitch together existing urban parcels, some of which may have legal encumbrances.[3] It seems so much simpler and straightforward to buy farmland at the edge and build a familiar housing subdivision. In the long run, however, this is a more costly strategy for everyone involved.

Chapter 7

Aerial photograph of Phoenix, Arizona. Photograph by Reid Ewing.

Fiscal Impact of Development

THE INEFFICIENCIES OF SPRAWLING DEVELOPMENT have become obvious for local governments trying to balance their budgets. Their attempts to collect enough revenue to provide services to residents, businesses, and workers fall short as they struggle to maintain aging infrastructure while also providing new roads, water and sewer lines, and other forms of developmental infrastructure. The increased costs end up being passed along to businesses and residents through higher taxes and fees, and sometimes through fewer public services. Sprawl's fiscal impact may be a major reason local governments have become so interested in more efficient forms of development.

Fiscal impact analysis measures how a jurisdiction will fare in the future as it raises revenues to meet its level of costs. On the revenue side of the ledger, the most significant revenue source is the property tax. Other taxes include levies on personal property, utility use, consumer products, and income. In addition to taxes, government jurisdictions receive income from interest earnings, permits, charges for services, fines and penalties, and so on. Nonlocal revenues include funding from the state and federal government. On the cost side of the ledger are operating, statutory, and capital costs, including police, fire, public works, general government, recreation, culture, and schools. Most of these costs are calculated at the county level; the county is also involved in the provision of public services, including health, welfare, incarceration, courts, parks, and roads.

Subtracting costs from revenues shows the net fiscal impact on a county. This is either a positive or a negative annual impact, which begins the day a development's structures are occupied and continues indefinitely until either the development or local fiscal factors are altered.[1]

For this analysis, data from the U.S. Census of Governments was used to determine public service costs per resident and per worker as well as revenues from real estate taxes and other sources. In both cases, costs and revenues were subdivided by whether they were associated with developed or undeveloped areas of the county. Tax rates and per-resident and per-worker costs were then applied to the projected new growth in the county, first for the sprawl scenario and then for the compact growth scenario.

Revenues and Costs

The nationwide annual revenues expected under sprawl conditions are $1,229 per capita and $537 per worker (Table 7.1). Two-thirds of per capita revenues come from the property tax; all of the per-worker revenues come from this source. Under the compact growth scenario, per-capita and per-resident revenues are slightly lower: $1,169 per capita and $533 per worker. About 70 percent of per-capita revenues come from the property tax, as do all per-worker revenues. In both cases, revenues per capita and per worker are 10 percent higher in the developed areas of each county and 20 percent lower in the undeveloped areas.

The total value of residential property (equalized valuation) per capita nationwide under the sprawl growth scenario amounts to $42,249; the value of property per worker is $30,349. This produces an equalized tax rate of about 20 mils, or $2 per $100 of equalized valuation (see Table 7.1). The tax rate under compact development is virtually the same, with slightly lower equalized valuation per capita of $39,452 for residential property and $29,745 per worker. By 2025,

TABLE 7.1
Fiscal Health under Sprawl and Compact Growth Scenarios (in Dollars)

	Developed Areas		Undeveloped Areas		Overall	
	Per Capita	Per Worker	Per Capita	Per Worker	Per Capita	Per Worker
Sprawl growth scenario						
Expenditures	2,473	129	1,833	92	2,267	120
Revenues						
Tax and nontax	997	607	692	362	894	537
Intergovernmental transfers	349	n/a	307	n/a	335	n/a
Total revenues	1,346	607	999	362	1,229	537
Equalized tax base	46,244	32,862	36,919	22,538	42,249	30,349
Equalized tax rate ($ per $100 value)	0.020		0.018		0.020	
Compact growth scenario						
Expenditures	2,388	125	1,729	87	2,203	117
Revenues						
Tax and nontax	912	585	592	355	825	533
Intergovernmental transfers	356	n/a	312	n/a	344	n/a
Total revenues	1,268	585	904	355	1,169	533
Equalized tax base	42,529	31,849	31,536	22,073	39,452	29,745
Equalized tax rate ($ per $100 value)	0.021		0.018		0.020	

Source: Center for Urban Policy Research, Rutgers University.

twenty-five years of revenues raised under sprawl growth conditions to support new development would amount to $99.4 billion annually. Overall revenues under the compact growth scenario would be expected to reach $99.5 billion annually. These revenues represent the sum of property tax, other revenues, and the funds from state and federal government. Revenues under the compact growth scenario are expected to be slightly higher annually than they would be under the sprawl growth scenario. This is a result of a combination of higher property taxes and somewhat lower property values in more densely built areas.

While revenues are expected to remain virtually the same, costs under the compact growth scenario are expected to be lower. This decrease in costs is possible because more development will take place in developed areas where public services may be more expensive, but the demand for public services can be absorbed more readily due to the excess capacity found there. Under conditions of sprawling growth, nationwide annual costs, averaged and weighted for the counties in which development takes place, are approximately $2,267 per capita and $120 per worker. Under compact growth, these costs are expected to be $2,203 per capita and $117 per worker. These average weighted county costs are about 10 percent higher per capita and per worker in the developed areas of each county and about 20 percent lower in the undeveloped areas (see Table 7.1).

While these differences in costs seem small—just $3 in the case of workers—they add up quickly, and they are due each year. The aggregate local cost of providing public services for all new residents and workers is approximately $143.2 billion annually by 2025 under sprawl growth conditions (Table 7.2). Overall costs generated by development under the compact growth scenario are expected to be $139.2 billion annually at build-out, or $4 billion less annually than under the sprawl scenario. This lower cost is seen in all four regions of the United States and reflects the servicing cost efficiencies of larger and more mature service providers under the controlled growth scenario.

These are the annual costs of providing the full array of local services—municipal, school district, and county—to new development. Annual costs under the controlled growth scenario reflect the differing development that will take place. More compact development will lower sewer, water, and road costs (as discussed in Chapter 5). Some studies have found that the operation and maintenance costs of these systems are also lower under more compact development.[2] Envision Utah, an ambitious project that examines several growth scenarios for the Greater Wasatch Front, found that the smart growth scenario favored by the public would save $4.5 billion in infrastructure costs through 2020.[3] Compact development would also allow more efficient provision of public services such as fire and police services. Fire, police, and emergency medical services must be positioned for rapid response, which in sprawl conditions means more stations and more personnel to cover spread-out development.

More compact growth may also lower school costs. Sprawling

TABLE 7.2

Annual Net Fiscal Impact under Sprawl and Compact Growth Scenarios, United States and by Region, 2000–2025 (in $ Million)

Region	Sprawl Growth Scenario			Compact Growth Scenario			Difference Compact Minus Sprawl
	Costs	Revenues	Impact	Costs	Revenues	Impact	
Northeast	9,329	11,170	1,841	9,252	12,928	3,676	1,835
Midwest	18,914	15,352	–3,562	18,340	16,339	–2,001	1,561
South	58,441	38,845	–19,532	57,655	39,062	–18,531	1,001
West	56,558	34,023	–22,535	53,942	31,215	–22,728	–192
United States	143,242	99,389	–43,788	139,190	99,544	–39,583	4,205

Source: Center for Urban Policy Research, Rutgers University.

development requires jurisdictions to build more school buildings, even as schools in former core areas lose students and deteriorate. The need to chase students as they move to the fringes of the metropolitan area leads to a revolving door of school construction and closings as well as the proliferation of classroom trailers and an increased need for busing. A study of two growth scenarios in Rhode Island found that a smart growth scenario could save the state $31 million out of $123 million in school costs.[4]

The Fiscal Impact of Sprawl Versus Compact Development

With all the revenues and costs calculated, under the sprawl growth scenario, development during the period 2000 to 2025 would be expected to cause an annual fiscal deficit of $43.8 billion, or 30 percent less revenues than costs by the final year of the projection period. This deficit is expected to occur in all regions except the Northeast, which has an expected positive fiscal impact of $1.8 billion annually. The Northeast has about the same cost structure per capita as the West, but revenues raised per capita are considerably more due to higher property taxes. The overall fiscal deficit is expected to be proportionally higher in the West and lower in the Midwest (see Table 7.2). The net fiscal impact under the compact growth scenario is also expected to be a deficit, but that deficit would be smaller—$39.6 billion annually—because while revenue is projected to remain virtually steady, costs are expected to decrease under this scenario. The compact growth scenario's fiscal impact is projected to reduce operating deficits to local governments by $4.2 billion annually by the time full build-out takes place in 2025.

Significant deficit reductions over sprawl growth are expected in every region except the West. These reductions will range from $1 billion in the South to $1.8 billion in the Northeast (see Table 7.2). In the West, an enhanced annual fiscal deficit of $192 million is expected under compact growth as the new population is faced with revenues and higher-cost service systems in developed portions of this region. Among Economic Areas, the thirty largest regions could reduce the deficit by $742 million annually with compact development. Nearly 60 percent of these regions would be able to reduce their fiscal deficits by embracing urban growth boundaries and urban service boundaries, with two notable exceptions: the greater Los Angeles region and the greater Washington, DC–Baltimore region are both projected to increase their deficits.

Conclusion

The fiscal deficit under the compact growth scenario is nearly 10 percent lower than the deficit projected under the sprawl growth scenario. This reduction results from greater use of the existing service structure in more densely developed areas. Real estate development and public service impacts are greater in locations where development is in a spread pattern and consists primarily of single-family homes. Lack of a variety of housing types and greater distances between similar housing types cause significant development and public service costs. These are compounded by insufficient non-property and existing property tax revenues; a deficit occurs that must be met by increasing local property tax revenues. Also, in more densely developed areas, the property tax may be slightly higher than it is in less densely developed areas; thus, revenues are expected to be proportionately higher.

In general, more compact development offers the prospect of deficit reductions as opposed to real cost savings for counties and other jurisdictions. This is because no matter what the form of development, growth is dominated by residential development that causes fiscal deficits under either scenario. Inexpensive single-family homes and other residences require the most services for the least tax dollars due to the need for schools and other residential services. More expensive homes and retail buildings offer more taxes for fewer services to municipalities and school districts, and industrial areas and office parks are sought after by (and sometimes provoke competition between) local cities or counties because they provide local governments with income from tax dollars while offering a limited need for services.[5]

Ironically, in many cases the argument for developing agricultural lands into housing subdivisions is that the new homes will expand the tax base. A series of "cost of community services" case studies conducted by the American Farmland Trust has consistently found that the taxes collected on farm and ranch land more than covered their costs, requiring just 36 cents in services for every dollar of revenue raised, compared to $1.15 in services for every dollar of revenue from residential development.[6]

More compact development in closer-in locations offers a greater variety of housing types that reduce housing costs to the consumer. Development in these areas also avails itself of higher tax rates and revenues, reducing the deficit of costs over revenues and providing less of an impact. While this analysis calculated these savings for the entire nation, a number of studies of regions and states have found that more compact growth patterns will help governments come closer to balancing their budgets. More compact development offers the benefit of reduced property development and public service costs.

Chapter 8

Watash Mountain Range, Salt Lake City, Utah. Photograph by Catherine Galley.

Travel and Congestion

ONE HALLMARK OF SPRAWLING DEVELOPMENT is the need to drive everywhere. That means traffic—and traffic congestion—which costs residents time and money. This analysis projects just how much travel savings new residents could expect under the compact growth scenario and whether more compact growth can alleviate traffic congestion.

The first step in determining travel costs is to calculate how much people travel under the two growth scenarios and then use that information to calculate total travel costs in dollar terms. The goal is to apply full per-mile costs to each person's travel so that comparisons can be made between the alternative scenarios of future growth. To do this, the model must distinguish between personal vehicles and transit use, because the costs of these modes vary; distance also must be expressed per person (rather than per vehicle) to create a common denominator between the modes. Rather than simply adding up the total costs of suburban versus urban travel, the model focuses on the costs faced by individuals with similar demographics in different counties due to sprawl or compact growth. As in the other parts of this book, the changes in travel and costs are calculated for the projected *growth* of travel; therefore, the projections do not take into account the potential for shifting travel patterns for current residents.

The primary source of information for the model is the Nation-wide Personal Transportation Survey (NPTS), a major study of travel patterns conducted every five or six years by the U.S. Bureau of Transportation Statistics.[1] This survey found that the majority of trips taken by Americans in 1995 were by privately owned vehicle (95 percent) and that only a small percentage of trips were taken by transit or by a combination of private vehicle and transit. Other modes, such as bicycling or walking, were not included in the analysis. These figures are consistent with trends observed over the past several decades of increased automobile use and increased suburbanization. Of the persons in this data set, only 39 percent are in households with children, and all but 11 percent are in the middle- and upper-income categories.

The models consider only the travel behavior of adults in metro-politan areas. Certainly, the effect of young children on an adult's travel decisions is important; for example, by some accounts, school drop-offs account for a large portion of morning rush hour traffic. This type of travel is captured by the NPTS.

This study begins with the premise that people who live in more compact areas are more likely to drive shorter distances and to take transit instead. This premise is supported by many studies showing that people who live in areas with higher densities and more transit service are less likely to climb into a car.[2]

This means that moving more people into more developed areas will likely affect people's travel patterns. Under the compact growth scenario, the model projects that approximately 4.4 million more people of driving age are expected to live in more developed areas than would be the case under the sprawl scenario. The model shifts new residents from outlying counties to more developed counties and also shifts residents to more developed areas within the counties where some were already expected to reside. Of these 4.4 million people of driving age, about 70 percent (3.2 million people) are

TABLE 8.1
Difference in Transit Use by New Residents Age Sixteen and Older
under Compact Growth Scenario, United States, 2000–2025

	Privately Owned Vehicle	Transit	Used Both	All
Sprawl growth scenario	45,417,270	2,066,009	989,357	48,472,636
Compact growth scenario	44,786,986	2,516,210	1,169,440	48,472,636
Difference	630,248 fewer	450,201 more	180,083 more	

Source: Woods & Poole (1998); Center for Urban Policy Research, Rutgers University.

expected to experience a change in density and other neighborhood attributes that would likely cause a change in their travel behavior. This would amount to approximately 6.5 percent of all future residents of driving age over the twenty-five-year projection period. (Table 8.1 shows the projected travel modes of all new residents under the two scenarios.) While the vast majority of trips would still be taken by private automobile, fewer people are expected to travel exclusively by private motor vehicle, while the number of residents who use transit exclusively or use both modes is expected to grow over the next twenty-five years.

Travel Patterns under Sprawl and Compact Growth Scenarios

Under the sprawl growth scenario, daily miles traveled in privately owned vehicles is expected to increase by 1.19 billion miles as a result of the travel of all new residents added between 2000 and 2025, most of which will occur in low-density areas where driving is a necessity (Table 8.2). The increase will amount to approximately 26 miles per person per day. Transit miles traveled daily will amount to 34.8 million miles, or 10 miles per person per day. This is a total of 1.23 billion travel miles per day.

Under the compact growth scenario, in which more people will live closer in and have access to transit, daily miles traveled in privately owned vehicles is expected to increase by 1.14 billion miles, or just under 25 miles per person per day. This is 4.7 percent lower than in the sprawl growth scenario, or nearly 56 million fewer miles trav-

TABLE 8.2

Difference in Transportation Miles and Costs under Compact Growth Scenario, United States, 2000–2025

	Privately Owned Vehicle Miles	Transit Miles	Total Travel Miles	Cost of Privately Owned Vehicle Miles	Cost of Transit Miles	Total Travel Costs
Sprawl growth scenario	1,193,526,000	34,842,000	1,228,368,000	$938,861,000	$47,746,000	$986,608,000
Compact growth scenario	1,137,329,000	41,479,000	1,178,809,000	$905,281,000	$57,256,000	$962,537,000
Difference	56,197,000 fewer	6,637,000 more	49,559,000 fewer	$33,581,000 less	$9,510,000 more	$24,071,000 less

Source: Woods & Poole (1998); Center for Urban Policy Research, Rutgers University.

FIGURE 8.1: NJ Transit bus in downtown New Brunswick, New Jersey. Photograph by Catherine Galley.

eled by automobile per day. On the other hand, transit miles traveled are expected to amount to 1.2 billion miles per day, or 11.3 miles per person per day. This is 19 percent higher than under the sprawl scenario, an increase of 6.6 million miles per day. Overall, the compact growth scenario is projected to result in 49.6 million fewer daily travel miles by the new residents.

Under the compact growth scenario, future settlements would be made more compact by adopting urban growth boundaries and urban service areas, which would focus more growth in a smaller area. The 2.6 million new residents expected to live in more compact communities are expected to generate less travel of all types simply because people who live close together do not need to travel as far.

Perhaps more important, the higher densities under the compact growth scenario would create the conditions necessary for successful, frequent transit service. Low density makes public transit inefficient, forcing a higher proportion of all ground movements to occur in private vehicles. Low density also discourages walking and bicycling trips and carpooling because it spreads people and their destinations over wider areas. Public transit vehicles cannot operate efficiently unless they can attain high loads because their patrons are concentrated together at either or both ends of the vehicles' trips. In 1995, in places with gross densities of from 1,000 to 4,000 persons per square mile, no bus service was available to 30.6 percent of households; in lower-density places, that fraction was 59 percent or higher.[3] Under the compact growth scenario, more new residents would live within range of convenient transit service.

While this national study analyzed only the influence of compactness on driving and transit use, other transportation research indicates that several other factors in the built environment also influence how people choose to travel.[4] A growing body of research shows that people will take more trips by foot or bicycle if their neighborhoods are walkable. Proximity of homes to shops, schools, or businesses increases the likelihood that residents will walk or bicycle, so higher-density areas with mixed-use development are expected to generate more walking trips and fewer car trips.[5] Walkable neighborhoods also offer good connectivity; they tend to have grid street patterns with more direct routes and with streets that provide for safe bicycling and walking.[6] An analysis of studies in six communities found that, on average, residents in highly walkable neighborhoods took twice as many walking trips as people in less walkable neighborhoods. Most of the increase was for performing errands or going to work.[7] Transit-oriented development (TOD) can also increase nonmotorized trips by grouping housing close to transit stops surrounded by shops and services. While the model for this study was not able to account for potential increases in walking trips, it bears noting that walking is the lowest-cost form of personal transportation.

One of the few U.S. regions with a long-standing urban growth boundary, Portland, Oregon, has also pursued a comprehensive strategy to create walkable neighborhoods and TOD. Atlanta, Georgia, is a metropolitan area that has expanded more rapidly than just about any urban area in the United States and has until recently focused its attention on expanding road capacity. A comparison of the change in the two cities' travel statistics from the mid-1980s to the mid-1990s demonstrates the potential of pursuing smart growth strategies. Portland's population grew by 26 percent during this time period, a bit lower than Atlanta's robust growth rate of 32 percent. The total vehicle miles traveled in Atlanta in this period grew by 17 percent, while in Portland it edged up just 2 percent. The number of people commuting in a single-occupancy vehicle dropped by 13 percent in Portland while growing by 15 percent in Atlanta. And while Atlanta was able to keep its commute times almost steady—growing just 1 percent—Portland's commute times dropped by 9 percent.[8] Portland's experience demonstrates how a compact growth strategy can help metropolitan areas alleviate increases in total miles traveled and percent travel in single occupancy vehicles.

Calculating the Costs of Travel

Determining the cost savings that may stem from the decrease in travel projected in the compact growth scenario requires an assessment of the fixed and variable costs of driving and taking transit, as well as a calculation of the monetary value of the time spent in a car, on a bus, or on a train.

THE COST OF DRIVING

The direct fixed costs of vehicle ownership are those that an individual or household incurs simply by owning a private vehicle, whether the vehicle is driven one mile, ten thousand miles, or twenty-five thousand miles per year. Fixed costs include the costs of financing or purchase, vehicle depreciation, and insurance. While depreciation and insurance may vary based on the daily or annual vehicle miles traveled and the location of the vehicle, the majority of these costs are fixed. The American Automobile Association (AAA) estimated that in 1995 the fixed costs of vehicle ownership for a private automobile were 41 cents per vehicle miles traveled (VMT), assuming ten thousand miles of driving per year. The present study uses this estimate but converts it to a cost per person miles traveled, for an estimated fixed cost of owning a car of about 26 cents a mile.

The direct variable costs of vehicle ownership are those associated with the operation of a vehicle. These costs include the cost of gasoline or diesel fuel, oil, tires, and normal vehicle repair and maintenance as well as short-term parking. Many factors affect these costs for an individual vehicle user. For example, the amount of fuel consumed during travel is directly related to the type, age, and mechanical condition of a vehicle. AAA estimates that in 1995 the variable cost of vehicle ownership was 9 cents per vehicle mile traveled. Transforming this cost to a basis of per person miles traveled in 1995 yields an estimate of 6 cents for all trips. The model also took into account the costs of parking at home, setting those costs at just under 3 cents per mile.[9] Vehicle owners also bear the costs of crashes through pain and suffering, lost time at work, and other costs not recoverable from insurance companies. These costs are set at 3 cents per mile.[10]

In addition to the costs incurred by vehicle owners, automobiles exact costs on governments and on society. The governmental costs include those not paid for by gas taxes, such as police and court system costs for traffic enforcement. Other costs borne by government include the value of free parking space provided on and off street, as well as some of the costs of crashes. Governmental costs are estimated at close to 6 cents per person mile traveled.

Societal costs reflect the cost of consuming common goods such as air or water and the cost related to air, land, or water pollution. These costs have generated much discussion, debate, and some disagreement on the accuracy of the estimated values and on their place in the public policy process. Parsons, Brinckerhoff, Quade, and Douglas, Inc. (PB) provides a set of environmental cost estimates that have been converted to a cost per person mile traveled for this analysis (Table 8.3).[11] Air pollution costs—as one of the most obvious external costs associated with the use of vehicles powered by internal combustion engines—are estimated at 0.029 cent per person mile traveled. Water pollution costs are attributed to a variety of sources, including leaking underground fuel tanks, large oil spills, contaminated urban runoff, and nitrogen deposition. Combining these costs, PB estimated water pollution costs at 0.001 cent per person mile traveled.

TABLE 8.3
Summary of Privately Owned Vehicle Travel Costs in Dollars/Per Mile Traveled (1995 $)

Privately Owned Vehicle Travel Costs	$/Per Mile Traveled for All Trips*
User costs	
Fixed costs of ownership	$0.258
Variable costs of ownership	$0.060
Internal parking costs	$0.027
Internal accident costs	$0.032
Subtotal	*$0.378*
Governmental costs	
Municipal costs	$0.006
External parking costs	$0.031
External accident costs	$0.023
Subtotal	*$0.059*
Social costs	
Air pollution	$0.029
Water pollution	$0.001
Noise pollution	$0.001
Climate change	$0.004
Subtotal	*$0.035*
Total cost per mile traveled	**$0.473**

Source: Parsons, Brinckerhoff, Quade, and Douglas, Inc.
*Subtotals may not add up due to rounding.

Noise pollution costs, which are quite localized, are somewhat harder to quantify. PB estimated the impact of noise pollution for different types of vehicles and different types of roads for a per-person mile estimate of 0.001 cent. A final social cost is the cost associated with climate change. It is estimated that automobiles produce as much as 30 percent of the total U.S. production of carbon dioxide responsible for global warming. Those costs are estimated at $0.035 cent per person mile traveled. The total social cost of automobiles used in this study is 0.473 cent per mile; when looking at costs just for work trips, total costs rise to almost 66 cents per mile (not shown).

THE COST OF TRANSIT

Travel costs per passenger mile for transit were also calculated based on two basic types of transit: bus and train travel. Rail transit includes commuter rail, heavy rail, and light rail. Bus transit includes motor bus and trolleybus.

The costs to users are obviously much lower under transit; this study estimated passenger per mile costs to be 19 cents based on information provided by the American Public Transit Association. These costs include base fares, zone and express service premiums, extra-cost transfers, and revenues paid by an organization (such as an employer) to provide transit for individuals. Using tax dollars, the government pays an estimated 36 cents per mile to operate transit lines, which includes the costs for operation and maintenance of vehicles and other infrastructure, general administration, and the purchase of private transportation. Operating costs are derived from the National Transit Database, which gives total costs for each transit agency. The social costs of transit—which include the costs of crashes as well as air, water, and noise pollution—are estimated to be quite low, about 1 cent per passenger mile. Capital costs—the costs of construction of the transit system and the purchase of the vehicles—are generally paid from federal, state, and local governments, at 10 cents per mile. For the purposes of this study, funds that are distributed to transit agencies by governments are considered to be government-incurred costs regardless of the original source of the funding (e.g., business or resident taxes). Total costs per passenger mile for transit are estimated at 66 cents.

While the cost of all trips is used to estimate the cost of travel via automobile and transit in this analysis, the cost of work trips bears noting because this class of trips produces the highest demand on the transportation system. The estimated cost of work trips by private vehicles is nearly the same as the estimated cost of transit trips. Since transit trips are predominantly work related, the cost of travel to work—when measured by person miles traveled—may be approximately the same regardless of travel mode.

A full accounting of the cost of travel must include estimates for the value of time spent traveling. The NPTS includes information about the number of minutes spent traveling for each automobile or transit trip taken. These data were used to create median travel time in minutes for urban, suburban, exurban, and rural residents based on whether they travel via personal vehicle, transit, or both.

Different estimates were determined for four income groups, and an average hourly wage was calculated for each group. The estimated number of minutes traveled by type of place and income group was converted to equivalent hours and multiplied by one-half the estimated hourly wage. This produced estimates of the value of time spent traveling according to income group and the type of place where residents lived.

THE COSTS OF TRAVEL UNDER THE TWO SCENARIOS

Using the figures described above for costs, daily travel costs under the sprawl growth scenario are expected to increase nationally by $986 million, or by more than 80 cents per person mile traveled. The increase in travel by automobile of 1.19 billion miles at 47 cents per mile each day leads to total personal, governmental, and societal costs of $563 million. The cost of travel time for these drivers and their passengers comes to $376 million daily, for total increased automobile travel costs of almost $939 million. Under the sprawl scenario, transit costs—including time costs—come to almost $48 million.

Under the compact growth scenario, the increase in total travel costs is expected to be somewhat lower because this scenario projects that people will travel about 56 million fewer miles each day. Total costs under compact growth are expected to be about $963 million. The cost of travel using privately owned vehicles, including time costs, is expected to grow to $905 million. Since transit use is projected to increase 19 percent over the sprawl growth scenario, total transit costs, including time, actually increase to $57 million. The cost per person mile traveled under this scenario is 81 cents per mile, slightly higher than under sprawl conditions because of the increase in transit use. (Remember that each mile of automobile travel was estimated at 47 cents and that each transit mile was estimated at 66 cents.) But this increase is more than offset by the overall decrease in miles traveled of almost 5 percent.

Costs for daily travel by privately owned vehicle for new residents are decreased by $33.6 million when the compact growth scenario is applied—a reduction of 3.6 percent. Transit daily travel costs are increased by $9.5 million, or 19.9 percent. Overall, daily travel costs are expected to be reduced by $24 million nationally, or 2.4 percent, under the compact growth scenario, using urban growth boundaries and urban service boundaries to manage growth. As discussed earlier in this chapter, other measures to design communities at a smaller scale to reduce automobile travel, including transit-oriented development and creation of walkable neighborhoods, could reduce travel by both new and existing residents. These measures are not accounted for in this calculation, but their potential indicates that travel and cost savings are likely to be higher than those estimated here.

Sprawl and Traffic Congestion

Often cited as part of the costs of sprawl are the costs of traffic congestion, as calculated annually by the Texas Transportation Institute (TTI). TTI's most recent estimate found that congestion costs 5.7 billion gallons of wasted fuel and 3.5 billion hours of lost productivity, for a total cost to the nation of $69.5 billion in 2001, $4.5 billion more than the previous year.

Congestion is probably the most widespread complaint about sprawl, especially in suburbs. Many residents and firms originally moved out of central cities and into suburbs partly to escape congested big-city conditions of all types. But as suburbs grew larger and more urbanized, the intense traffic congestion followed these "refugees." Resentment against travel delays is one of the most powerful forces underlying the rise of the entire smart growth movement. But while more compact growth can undoubtedly reduce *automobile travel,* as demonstrated above, it may not be able to substantially reduce *traffic congestion,* particularly peak-hour traffic congestion.

The most obvious causes of rising congestion in the suburbs of U.S. metropolitan regions have been increased population and the increase in driving. From 1990 to 1998, the total suburban population of the nation's metropolitan areas increased by 12.5 percent, whereas all the central cities grew by only 3.9 percent. Vehicle travel in the

United States has been rising even more steeply than population because of more widespread vehicle ownership and more intensive usage per vehicle. From 1980 to 2000, the number of cars and trucks registered increased by 42 percent and the number of miles driven *per vehicle* increased by 28 percent, whereas total population increased by only 24 percent. The total number of miles traveled by all motor vehicles annually soared by 80 percent between 1980 and 2000. Because most of the population growth in U.S. metropolitan areas from 1980 to 2000 took place in the suburbs, most of the expansion of auto ownership, usage, and miles driven was also generated by vehicles owned by suburban residents and occurred within the suburbs.

To some extent, worsening traffic congestion in the suburbs was an inevitable result of the rapid growth of population, vehicle ownership, and vehicle usage there. No matter what spatial form suburban growth took in that period, it would surely have generated rising congestion throughout most suburbs.

Some observers claim that the low average density of most suburban growth during the past several decades—that is, sprawl—made the resulting traffic congestion much worse than it would have been if suburban growth had occurred at higher densities. The combination of longer trips and high proportions of movers using private vehicles undoubtedly results in many more miles driven on the roads each day than would occur if people lived in higher-density settlements.

But more compact developments would not necessarily result in lower traffic congestion than sprawl developments do. Repeated studies conducted by TTI show decisively that traffic has become more congested in almost all metropolitan areas during the past two decades. TTI's studies do not differentiate between suburban and in-city degrees of congestion. And although some observers believe TTI's measures of congestion are flawed, they are the most comprehensive, consistent, and widely applied measures available and are often quoted by media and elected officials. An analysis of one of TTI's measures of congestion, the travel time index (a ratio between the time it takes to drive a given route during peak travel periods and the time it takes to drive the same route when there is no congestion), found that—other factors being equal—higher gross settlement density generates worse congestion. Conversely, urbanized areas with larger territory apparently spread traffic out and thus reduce congestion.

Workplaces and shopping facilities in low-density settlements are spread out more than those in high-density settlements. So commuters in the former areas do not converge on such a small number of destinations—thereby generating congestion there—as they do in the latter. Average commuting times tend to be shorter among rural residents than among metro-area residents.[12] This is for three reasons: (1) rural commuters travel some of their journeys over relatively uncongested roads, so they can attain higher average speeds than most metro-area commuters, offsetting their longer commutes; (2) a higher fraction of central city metro workers commute by public transit, which normally takes longer than moving in private vehicles; and (3) most rural, outer-suburban dwellers also work in the same areas, so fewer have to pass through crowded in-city arteries. Thus, it is not clear that sprawling, low-density settlements generate worse congestion than higher-density areas, though the former certainly generates more travel per household.

TRIPLE CONVERGENCE

Many measures designed to reduce congestion, including adding travel lanes or shifting travelers to public transit, would probably have limited success due to the principle of *triple convergence.* Using an expansion of one region's transit system as an example, it seems obvious that expanding transit facilities serving that region would surely cause some commuters to move off the region's roads during peak hours. But the initial movement of even a large number of vehicle commuters off heavily congested roads onto transit during peak hours probably would not reduce peak-hour congestion on those roads, because nearly every initial peak-hour commuter who shifted *off* those roads onto transit would soon be replaced by another vehicle commuter moving *onto* the same roads during the same peak hours. These travelers would take advantage of the less congested roadway, moving from other road routes, other times, or other travel modes. As a result, the average level of congestion on those roads during peak hours would not decline. This phenomenon is called the principle of triple convergence, and its validity has been confirmed by experiences all over the world.[13]

The principle of triple convergence springs from the strongly interdependent relations among different elements of the ground transportation networks within each region. Every major expressway is part of a much larger network of roads, streets, transit facilities, and other expressways within its region. Most travelers have two or more options concerning which routes, times, and modes of movement they can use to reach their daily destinations at the appropriate times. They choose the routes, times, and modes that optimize their personal combinations of convenience, travel time, and discomfort. Under any given conditions, all of these diverse travelers arrive at a type of overall equilibrium about how, when, and where they will travel each day. However, any major change in the initial conditions may cause many travelers to adjust their choices about which modes, routes, and times they select—thereby changing the system's equilibrium.

In one respect, more compact future settlements might reduce future traffic congestion. The total amount of future vehicle travel in metropolitan fringe areas would be much greater if large portions of those areas were settled at very low densities—say, below 1,000 persons per square mile (about 1.2 housing units per net residential acre)—rather than at moderate densities—say, more than 2,500 persons per square mile (about 2.9 housing units per net residential acre). In the former case, so much more vehicle travel would occur than in the latter case that congestion might be more intense at major arterial intersections. Preventing very low fringe densities in outlying portions of metropolitan areas might reduce future traffic congestion there, compared to allowing completely unchecked sprawl.

Summary

Shifting most future growth from continued sprawl to much higher density and more compact forms—however desirable that may be for many reasons—is not likely to notably reduce future levels of peak-hour traffic congestion, compared to continued sprawl. Of course, the lower total travel springing from higher-density and more compact settlements would produce other benefits, including lower total fuel consumption and, possibly, less air pollution.

Several studies have shown that a number of strategies can improve the overall performance of the transportation system. Street connectivity, a walkable environment, shorter route options, and more transit service improve the functioning of the network.[14] Traffic management techniques can help slow the growth of congestion, while transit can provide more people with the choice to get away from it. But perhaps the most optimistic way to look at the inability to eliminate traffic congestion is to see it as a sign of success: it indicates economic activity and serves as a necessary balancing mechanism for a transportation system that could never be built to accommodate all peak-hour travel without delays.

Chapter 9

Street festival, Princeton, New Jersey. Photograph by Anton Nelessen.

Quality-of-Life Consequences

SUPPORTERS OF SMART GROWTH argue that sprawling development is exacting a cost on Americans by degrading their quality of life. Opponents say that Americans have spread out because they want to—and that having people live in more dense settlements will damage Americans' already high quality of life. Who is right? Quality of life is, of course, notoriously difficult to quantify and measure, but by looking at individual aspects of the issue we can draw some conclusions.

This chapter looks first at whether a standardized index of quality of life shows any change between the sprawl and compact development scenarios presented in this book. Then it considers individual issues related to quality of life, particularly health and sense of community. Some quality-of-life benefits of sprawl are also discussed in Chapter 11.

Quality-of-Life Index

If a household could be moved from a sprawl county to a more compact location in a nonsprawling county (as defined in earlier chapters), would its quality of life change? If all households were moved, how might the change in quality of life be significant for society?

Magazines have become famous for producing a variety of

indices measuring quality of life. Such rankings of the best places to live and the best places to raise children are issued regularly, usually with a mix of objective and subjective categories and sometimes using results submitted by readers. A strong desire for an overall index of quality of life exists. This chapter uses a rigorous quality-of-life index to estimate the value of changes in the quality of life experienced by new residents under the two alternative development futures—sprawling growth and more compact growth—for the United States.

One widely used model for estimating the value of the quality of life associated with location was developed by Stuart Gabriel of the University of Southern California and his colleagues.[1] Gabriel's model compares quality of life in one state to another and uses it to predict housing costs and wages in relation to the amenities of each location—in this case, counties. To use Gabriel's index for this study, the variables were altered and supplemented to achieve recognizable indicators.[2]

The twenty-six variables influencing overall quality of life are presented in Table 9.1, which also indicates whether they are positively or negatively associated with a good quality of life. For counties that contain only undeveloped or developed areas, all twenty-six variables were used to determine the quality of life in that jurisdiction. For counties that contain both developed and undeveloped areas, thirteen variables were used to describe the quality of life in developed areas and thirteen variables were used to describe the quality of life in undeveloped areas. This is due to the absence of below-county-level data for all variables. A combined county score was then calculated, weighted to reflect the relative populations in developed and undeveloped areas.

The indicators that appear here are coarse, representing just one moment in time, and are often subjective. Most of the indicators are not directly influenced by development (such as weather), and the few variables that might be affected by development (such as air pollution) have not been adjusted to account for potential differences. A jurisdiction's quality of life is the summation of the quality-of-life

TABLE 9.1
Variables Used in the Quality-of-Life Ranking of Counties

Variable	Developed (D) or Undeveloped (U) Areas	Correlation between Variable and Quality of Life	Weighting
1. Average annual rainfall	U	−	1
2. Morning and evening humidity	U	−	1
3. Heating degree days	U	−	1
4. Cooling degree days	U	−	1
5. Wind speed	U	−	1
6. Sunshine days	U	+	1
7. Coast location	U	+	.25
8. Inland water bodies	U	+	1
9. Hazardous waste sites	D	−	.25
10. Commuting time	D	−	1
11. Violent crime rate	D	−	1
12. Air content—ozone	D	−	1
13. Air content—carbon monoxide	D	−	.25
14. Student-teacher ratio	U	−	.25
15. State and local income taxes	D	−	1
16. State and local property taxes	U	−	1
17. State and local sales taxes	D	−	1
18. Expenditures on higher education	D	−	.25
19. Expenditures on public welfare	D	−	1
20. Expenditures on highways	D	−	.25
21. Wealth index	U	+	1
22. Working age population	D	+	1
23. Population with a graduate degree	D	+	1
24. Cost-of-living index	U	−	1
25. Population growth	U	≈+	.25
26. Employment growth	D	≈+	.25

Source: Center for Urban Policy Research, Rutgers University.
Note: A (+) sign indicates a positive correlation between the variable and quality of life; a (−) sign indicates a negative correlation between the variable and quality of life; a (≈+) sign indicates that for population growth and employment growth a positive correlation exists between the variable and quality of life except for extreme high growth, which is given a middle rating. In counties that are typified either by all undeveloped areas (2,450 counties) or by all developed areas (160 counties), all twenty-six variables are used for quality of life. In counties that contain both developed and undeveloped areas (490 counties), thirteen variables are used for their developed areas and thirteen variables are used for their undeveloped areas. Again, all twenty-six variables are used to define quality of life in a county.

variables as experienced by new residents. Quality-of-life scores for each county were multiplied by the number of people expected to move there. In each scenario, the overall quality of life is the same; the difference is the number of people who experience it in different places. This is meant to be not an exercise in extreme precision or classification but rather a comparison of impacts under alternative growth scenarios.

Using the modified Gabriel quality-of-life index, quality of life for new residents in the United States under the sprawl growth scenario averages 3.00 on a scale of 0 to 6, right at the middle of the scale (Table 9.2). For developed areas, the quality-of-life rating averaged 8 percent higher (3.11) than the quality-of-life rating for undeveloped areas (2.85). The lowest overall value of quality of life is found in the Midwest (2.87), followed by the South (2.92) and the Northeast (2.95). The quality-of-life rating in the West is 3.20, which is 9 percent higher than the rating for the Northeast and the South and 11 percent higher than that for the Midwest. Western locations typically get high marks for quality of life due to the wealth of their areas, education of their population, mild weather, lower crime rates, lower taxes, and manageable levels of population and job growth. Midwestern locations get lower marks because of their more extreme weather conditions, higher taxes and crime rates, and very slow growth rates or actual decline. Northeastern locations get lower marks than the West for reasons similar to the Midwest but do slightly better in the growth and weather categories. The South gets lower marks than the West primarily due to lower wealth and education levels, hot weather, and in some cases, extreme levels of population and employment turnover.

Under the compact growth scenario, the quality-of-life score for the nation as a whole is identical—approximately 3.0 (see Table 9.2). The obvious conclusion is that pursuing a more compact development pattern in metropolitan areas to channel growth results in virtually no change in overall quality of life for new residents at the national level. However, changes at the regional level do occur. This is particularly true of developed areas in the four U.S. regions. Those who are expected to live in the developed areas of the Northeast, Midwest, and South under the compact growth regimen will experience a slight decrease in their quality of life. Under compact growth, more people will be heading to developed areas and fewer will be heading to areas with better rankings.

TABLE 9.2
Quality-of-Life Index for New Residents under Sprawl and Compact Growth Scenarios (by Region)

Region	Sprawl Growth Scenario			Compact Growth Scenario			Difference between Compact and Sprawl Growth Scenarios		
	Developed	Undeveloped	All*	Developed	Undeveloped	All*	Developed	Undeveloped	All*
Northeast	3.15	2.75	2.95	3.11	2.79	2.94	–0.04	0.03	–0.01
Midwest	3.12	2.65	2.87	3.09	2.67	2.86	–0.03	0.02	0.00
South	3.02	2.78	2.92	3.00	2.79	2.91	–0.02	0.01	0.00
West	3.19	3.15	3.19	3.21	3.14	3.21	0.02	–0.01	0.01
United States	3.11	2.85	3.00	3.10	2.85	3.01	–0.01	0.00	0.00

Source: Center for Urban Policy Research, Rutgers University.
*May vary slightly from straight subtraction due to rounding.

In contrast, those who will live in the developed areas of the West will experience a slight increase in their quality of life, because developed areas in this region are strong economically and otherwise. The primary and secondary cities of the western divisions are much healthier than their southern, midwestern, and northeastern counterparts. For undeveloped areas, quality of life will increase slightly for those who move to these locations in the Northeast, Midwest, and South because fewer people are going to these locations and those who do are locating in the more desirable undeveloped areas. Under the compact growth scenario, the most extreme areas—those with the lowest populations and less sophisticated services and infrastructure—are being avoided. These are the areas where follow-up land preservation may be possible. There will be a very slight decrease in quality of life in undeveloped areas in the West because some of the undeveloped areas are closer in and less desirable than the extreme and more pristine outer areas, which are no longer targeted under alternative development.

The basic message is that, in the aggregate, overall quality of life experienced by new residents in the United States would be unaltered as a result of the compact growth scenario. The very small changes that do occur represent a small decrease in quality of life in regions other than the West and a small increase in quality of life in the West. These slight changes are due to the relative health of central cities in these regions.

This analysis shows that a scenario in which 25 percent of new growth is moved to more compact areas would not appreciably affect quality of life for those new residents. We now turn to a more general discussion of some quality-of-life issues affected by development.

Individual Quality-of-Life Issues

It could be argued that many of the earlier chapters of this book have also dealt with quality-of-life issues; traffic congestion, housing affordability, concentration of poverty, and access to open space all affect everyday quality of life. However, this section concentrates on the quality-of-life costs that are most difficult to measure and for which a thorough national analysis of the two growth scenarios was simply not possible.

HEALTH

One quality-of-life cost of sprawl is how sprawl affects personal health. The potential health impacts that have gotten the most attention are sprawl's effect on physical activity, pedestrian danger, respiratory health through air pollution, and stress.

Physical Activity

Several recently released studies have found that people who live in more sprawling areas are likely to get less physical activity and are more likely to be obese or overweight than people who live in more compact places. One study that evaluated sprawl and health in 448 metropolitan area counties using a version of the Smart Growth America sprawl index found that for every fifty-point increase in the degree of sprawl, the average resident was likely to be one pound heavier.[3] Residents of sprawling areas were also more likely to have hypertension, and they walked less. A study that analyzed the neighborhood within a kilometer of participants' homes in the Atlanta region found that people who had more destinations within walking distance were considerably less likely to be obese and that they walked more and drove less. The study also found that every half-hour increase in time spent in a car each day increased the likelihood of obesity by 3 percent.[4]

In contrast, a number of studies have found that people who live in walkable communities take more trips on foot, enough to keep off one pound per year.[5] Since people living in more sprawling areas drive more and have fewer alternate travel options, they also have fewer opportunities to get healthy physical activity as part of everyday life—what is known as "active living."

Physical inactivity clearly influences obesity and also plays a role in a host of diseases, including diabetes, colon cancer, and high blood pressure. Physical inactivity is linked to more than two hundred thousand deaths each year, and some public health officials believe that obesity may soon overtake smoking as the nation's number one health problem. The cost of treating obesity, chronic diseases, and other conditions associated with physical inactivity is estimated at $77 billion per year.[6]

Pedestrian Danger

While walking clearly has health benefits, sprawl also has been accused of making it more difficult and dangerous to walk. More pedestrians die in places where more people walk, but when exposure is controlled for, sprawling metropolitan areas have proven more dangerous for pedestrians because of their wide, high-speed arterial streets and lack of sidewalks and safe crossings.[7]

Respiratory Health

Some observers have connected sprawling development to poor respiratory health because the increased driving required by sprawl means higher levels of air pollution. Although emission controls have reduced tailpipe emissions, increased driving has offset that benefit. Automobiles produce more than half of carbon monoxide emissions and about a third of oxides of nitrogen and volatile organic compounds, precursors to the formation of ground-level ozone pollution.[8] Such pollutants aggravate respiratory illness, increase respiratory infections, and cause decreased lung function and lung inflammation. Recent research indicates that ozone pollution may also influence the development of asthma in children. In addition, the tiny particles that fall off tires and brake linings, as well as road dust kicked up by cars, are a significant source of particulate pollution, which has been associated with increased hospital admissions and premature death among vulnerable populations.[9]

Researchers have analyzed the air pollution costs per mile driven, which range from 1 to 8 cents per mile. A recent analysis by Litman estimated 5 cents per mile for urban peak travel and 4 cents per mile for off-peak travel, taking into account both tailpipe emissions and particulate pollution.[10]

An analysis using the Smart Growth America metropolitan sprawl index found that metropolitan areas with a higher degree of sprawl experienced more maximum ozone days, and that this outweighed the effect of all other variables tested.[11] That study, as well as the analysis in this book, found that sprawling development is linked to more miles traveled via automobile. However, an analysis of New Jersey air quality using an earlier version of the sprawl and compact growth models used in this book found that air pollution reductions would be almost the same under sprawling or compact growth scenarios, due in large part to more stringent emission controls.[12]

Stress

A few studies have emphasized the stress cost of commuting. Again, the allegation here is that more time spent in an automobile exerts a stress cost, which includes effects on blood pressure, tolerance for frustration, and negative mood. Some studies have found that when the commute is impeded by traffic congestion or other factors, stress levels increase.[13]

SENSE OF COMMUNITY

A "cost" of development that is truly impossible to measure is how much a neighborhood, town, or city contributes to or denies people a sense of place and community. Although it is hard to define, writer Tony Hiss argues that the experience of place has a profound impact on people's lives and deserves close, sustained attention.[14] William Whyte pioneered the idea that public places have social value, and the group Project for Public Spaces continues his work. A few studies have explored the impact of sprawl on sense of place by exploring aesthetic concerns, the presence of cultural activities, and strength of community bonds. Seventy percent of the Baby-Boom Generation will retire in-place. Their familiarity with and love of a place are the reasons they will remain there.

FIGURE 9.1: A parking lot in downtown Phoenix, Arizona. Photograph by Catherine Galley.

Aesthetic Concerns

Some writers have argued that sprawl is simply ugly—that huge signs lining wide arterial roads in front of strip shopping centers create a landscape that people find displeasing and even stressful. Diamond and Noonan, in *Land Use in America,* found that a growing portion of suburbanites are faced with "real burdens on the texture, continuity, and depth of social life, as well as on the diversity, beauty, and health of the surrounding landscape."[15] Visual preference surveys and other tools that have people choose the most appealing of two images find that people consistently choose areas with more "smart growth" attributes. A recent national study using this technique found that 60 percent of respondents did not like mass-produced suburban subdivisions in rural areas.[16] However, low-density developments are not all the same, and some low-density residential developments, particularly high-income ones, have attractive open space and elaborate landscape designs, whereas many urban neighborhoods lack green space and can be singularly unattractive. Thus this cost of sprawl remains unproven.

A related cost of sprawl is that historic structures may be more likely to deteriorate and be torn down in sprawling conditions. According to Constance Beaumont, formerly of the National Trust for Historic Preservation, the concentration of poverty and disinvestment in urban areas, where historic buildings are concentrated, means more of those buildings are left empty and subject to deterioration. The widening of roads to accommodate increased automobile traffic, combined with the expansiveness of suburban subdivisions, increases the likelihood that historic structures will be razed.[17]

Another aspect of quality of life that is a function of place is the presence of cultural amenities, such as live theater and other arts. Such amenities are more easily supported and more prevalent in dense urban cores and have been cited as one factor driving the revitalization of many urban neighborhoods.

Social Capital and Social Connections

In 1961, when Jane Jacobs wrote the first book to condemn sprawl, *The Death and Life of Great American Cities*, one of her primary arguments for the value of urban neighborhoods was the value of social interaction.[18] More recently, researchers have examined whether sprawling development has directly weakened a sense of community or depleted social capital. A sense of community is defined as a feeling of membership, influence, and integration into a neighborhood in which residents believe their needs can be met and where they share an emotional connection.[19] Social capital is the value of social networks in which people do things for one another based on reciprocity.

Opponents of sprawl claim that low-density development weakens households' connections to neighbors and the larger community. Neighbors are believed to be isolated from one another due to a heavy reliance on automobile travel and the lack of neighborhood retail outlets or other gathering places where they might meet. In addition, long commutes reduce the amount of time people might have for social interaction. In *Bowling Alone,* Robert Putnam estimated that every additional ten minutes spent commuting results in a 10 percent drop in civic engagement.[20]

A recent survey of studies that compared sense of community in New Urbanist and traditional neighborhoods found that several studies documented an increase in sense of community, chance encounters with neighbors, and civic engagement.[21] However, the study noted that self-selection and other factors might skew the results. Some studies showed mixed results. One showed increased neighborliness—informal interaction with neighbors—but found no increase in the overall sense of community as rated on a twelve-item scale. Another study, of Kentlands, Maryland, found higher participation in community activities but no greater sense of caring for neighbors.

Conclusion

Quality of life is very personal. No doubt many Americans feel they get a high quality of life from their sprawling communities, while others prefer more compact and diverse neighborhoods. The national analysis using the quality-of-life index suggests that overall quality of life would not be greatly affected if the compact growth scenario were to become reality. In looking at individual factors, sprawl's negative impact on health through constriction of physical activity and increased air pollution appears to be a serious cost, reaching billions of dollars. The evidence on sense of place and community is less conclusive but points to the possibility that the decline of civic and community life may be a cost of sprawl. Chapter 11 reviews some of the benefits of sprawl, many of which fall into the quality-of-life category. Weighing the costs and benefits is important in determining once and for all whether future sprawl or future compact growth would improve Americans' lives. Always remember the most important thing—neither alternative is mutually exclusive. The compact growth alternative has much of its development in sprawl locations. The sprawl growth alternative has a portion of its growth in central city redevelopment.

Chapter 10

A deteriorated structure before revitalization, Atlantic City, New Jersey. Photograph by Catherine Galley.

Sprawl, Urban Decline, and Social Policy

SUBURBAN SPRAWL exerts two types of costs on American society. The first consists of directly growth related costs, mainly in the suburbs. These include many of the costs detailed in earlier chapters, such as traffic congestion, air pollution, "excessive" absorption of farmlands and other open space, and high infrastructure costs. Such costs have aroused great antipathy toward sprawl, mainly from suburban residents, environmentalists, and urban planners.

The second type of costs attributed to sprawl spring from disinvestment in core urban areas and the concentration of poverty in inner-core parts of cities and older suburbs. As the suburbs have captured most employment and population growth, urban areas and inner-ring suburbs have been left to grapple with aging infrastructure, a shrinking population and tax base, and a concentration of citizens with the greatest needs.

According to Bruce Katz of the Brookings Institution, this imbalance in metropolitan growth contributes to traffic congestion, lost economic opportunities, fiscal strain, and trouble for low-income minority families.[1] Areas without vibrant cores may be missing out on opportunities for growth, because cities foster a high level of social exchange among diverse people and offer a chance for business innovation. In addition, they offer cultural amenities valued by highly skilled workers whether they live in the city or the suburbs. The fiscal strains associated with the imbalance in metropolitan growth have already been discussed (see Chapters 5 and 7): jurisdictions in core neighborhoods struggle to provide services and preserve aging infrastructure, while suburban governments can barely keep up with the need for brand-new infrastructure and services in far-flung neighborhoods. But perhaps the starkest cost of this imbalance is the concentration of low-income minority families in troubled neighborhoods.

The Costs of Concentrating Poverty

Neighborhoods where poverty is concentrated contain only a small percentage of the U.S. population, but they are rife with four virulent problems undermining social cohesion and economic efficiency throughout the nation: high rates of crime and violence, high percentages of children growing up in poverty, poor-quality public education, and the failure to integrate people into the mainstream workforce. Conditions in such areas do not provide people living there with life opportunities anywhere near those available to people living in nonpoverty areas, especially affluent suburbs. The result is an inequality of opportunity that disadvantages millions of Americans, especially young children. Either directly or indirectly, these problems affect every community in the nation, large and small.

Political economist Paul Jargowsky has calculated that, in 2000, there were 2,510 census tracts in U.S. metropolitan areas where at least 40 percent of the residents had incomes below the official poverty level. These concentrated poverty areas were home to about 7.9 million people. This was only 2.8 percent of the nation's total population in 2000 but represented more than 23 percent of the nation's poor people.[2] The number of poor persons living in these concentrated poverty areas dropped by 2.3 million—or 24 percent—from 1990 to 2000. The numbers of both whites and African Americans in these areas fell substantially, but the number of Hispanics rose slightly. Consequently, 76 percent of the residents of these neighborhoods were members of minority groups—mainly African Americans (39 percent) and Hispanics (29 percent). The lack of skills, energy, jobs, and economically productive performance of many of these people creates a serious enough handicap to the American economy to affect the welfare of almost everyone in the long run.

The long period of general prosperity from 1991 to 2000 notably reduced the severity of concentrated poverty in big cities. While the number of people living in such neighborhoods doubled between 1970 and 1990, it dropped by one-quarter in the 1990s. Moreover, the share of all poor African Americans living in such neighborhoods dropped from 30 percent in 1990 to 19 percent in 2000. In addition, the national rate of serious crimes per 100,000 U.S. residents fell 29.7 percent from its recent peak in 1991 to its lowest level in 2001. A very tight labor market in the late 1990s made it possible for many more low-skilled workers to become integrated into the mainstream workforce. The percentage of American children under age eighteen being reared in poverty also declined, from its recent peak of 22 percent in 1993 to 16.7 percent in 2001.

In spite of these improvements during the 1990s, the ill effects of continuing inner-city poverty concentrations still represent a major social problem for America as a whole. Crime remains significantly higher in urban areas, and many other indicators of social health did not improve as markedly in urban areas as they did in the suburbs. More than 16 percent of American children—and close to one out of two in concentrated poverty areas—are still reared in poverty. Rising unemployment from 2000 through 2003 offset many of the inner-city job gains achieved during the 1990s. The low quality of public education in big cities did not measurably improve in the 1990s, nor has it since. Hence it is critical to understand how, and to what extent, the American metropolitan growth process contributes to continuing poverty concentrations—and therefore to urban decline in major cities.

It has generally been believed that sprawl is a significant cause of concentrated urban poverty. This belief is based on the fact that several of the traits used to define sprawl seem likely to aggravate

urban decline. Very low density residential and nonresidential development spreads an entire metropolitan area out over a much larger
territory than it would occupy if densities were higher. This separates
many low-income households and unemployed workers living in
core areas from peripheral job opportunities. It also makes widespread use of public transit impractical—making it difficult for
people too poor to own their own vehicles to reach jobs and services.
The unlimited outward expansion of new growth and leapfrog development permits the construction of new subdivisions far out into
vacant land, eventually drawing new places of employment into
areas beyond the commuting range of most unemployed inner-city
residents.

In addition, the small, fragmented governments characteristic of
sprawling areas permit communities to engage in exclusionary zoning. These conditions prevent many low-income households from
living near where new jobs are being created in new-growth suburbs,
thereby helping concentrate poor residents in inner-city neighborhoods. Government fragmentation means local officials have no
incentive to take into account the impact of their parochial actions
on the region as a whole. A lack of coordinated regional planning
exacerbates this problem. Fragmented control over the tax base also
causes local governments in older cities and some inner-ring suburbs
to lose access to taxable resources that move outside their boundaries, even if the households and firms that have moved out continue
to use services provided by those city governments.

The Relationship between Sprawl and Urban Decline

However, merely asserting that these causal relationships seem
likely does not prove that they actually exist or—if they do—that they
contribute significantly to urban decline. One analysis of the relationship between measures of urban decline and measures of sprawl
found only weak relationships. The analysis defined urban areas as
in decline if their central cities lost population from 1980 to 1990
or if they received a low score in an index that included the rate of

violent crime, percentage of city residents below the poverty line, median household income, unemployment rate, high school graduation rate, and related factors. It found no statistically meaningful linkage between any measure of suburban sprawl and the percentage rate of change in central city populations from 1980 to 1990.[3]

Some statistically significant linkages do exist between three specific measures of sprawl elements and the index of urban decline. Urbanized areas with a high ratio of central city poverty to suburban poverty, with a lower portion of the total population living in the central city, or with a greater number of local governments with zoning powers, all were more likely to have higher scores on the scale of urban decline.[4] However, even these three statistically significant linkages are extremely weak because it would take implausibly large changes in each of the measures to produce any notable change in the urban decline index. Hence the data do not support those hypothesized causal linkages between sprawl and urban decline.

If sprawl is not the primary cause of urban decline, what is causing cities to suffer? Sprawl has so dominated American metropolitan growth for the past half century that many observers think sprawl and the entire growth process are one and the same thing—but that is not true. The underlying growth process has several important traits besides those that define sprawl, and many of those other traits would still be in effect even if growth occurred in much more compact forms. These other nonsprawl traits may be more important causes of concentrated inner-city poverty than any of the traits that define sprawl.

Several fundamental traits of metropolitan growth that are found in most suburban development in the United States are not inherent parts of sprawl. These traits, which influence urban decline, include high-quality standards for new construction, an unwillingness to subsidize low-income housing, racial segregation in housing, continuous immigration from abroad, exclusionary zoning, and a bias toward growth on vacant peripheral land.

The requirement that all new housing and other construction— wherever it is located—meet high-quality standards of design, size, and materials means that these structures often become too expensive for low-income households to occupy without subsidies. At the same time, federal, state, or local legislatures generally refuse to provide enough housing subsidies for most low-income households to occupy new units. Another trait functioning independently of sprawl is racial segregation: most white households are unwilling to live in neighborhoods where more than one-third of the residents are African Americans. A final factor that can contribute to a concentration of poverty is the ongoing inflows into U.S. metropolitan areas of large numbers of relatively low-income households from outside the nation, who often make such poor neighborhoods their first homes in the United States.

Two other growth traits that contribute to urban decline are related at least indirectly to sprawl. Suburban governments often deliberately adopt exclusionary zoning policies designed to make it difficult or impossible for low-income households to live in such communities. While this last trait is not inherent to sprawl, the fragmentation of governance that is a fundamental trait of sprawl makes instituting these policies easier. In addition, financing systems that favor standardized, sprawl-style development products, such as residential subdivisions and office parks, help fuel the bias toward growth at the edge of existing communities rather than redeveloping properties in older built-up areas.

The American metropolitan growth process definitely aggravates urban decline—but sprawl is not necessarily the main culprit. Other more fundamental elements of that growth process influence urban decline, only two of which are closely related to a defining trait of sprawl. Therefore, future policies designed to alleviate urban decline should focus on changing one or more of the fundamental traits in the American metropolitan growth process rather than solely on changing the elements that compose sprawl.

In addition to traits of the growth process, urban decline has been fueled by state and federal policies that have lowered the costs of development on the fringe of regions while increasing the costs of investment in built-up areas.[5] Policies that reduce the costs of fringe development include transportation investments weighted toward investment at the fringe of metropolitan areas as well as the home mortgage deduction, which favors higher-income suburban areas. On the other hand, federal policies make urban investment more expensive by making cleaning up environmental hazards in urban areas too expensive; also, until very recently, federal public housing investments were adding to the concentration of poverty by putting more public housing in already poor areas.

Conclusion

Viewed realistically, total elimination of poverty concentrations from all large, older American cities will not occur in the foreseeable future. Continuing immigration of poor households from abroad will constantly replenish the ranks of those residing in such concentrations. The wage structure of the America economy is such that even millions of full-time workers do not earn enough to lift themselves and their families out of severe poverty without public assistance.

Yet the American public has not been willing to provide enough such assistance to raise all of these families out of poverty. As long as the conditions described above persist, at least hundreds of thousands, and perhaps millions, of American households will have incomes too low to support occupancy of housing units considered minimally "decent" by prevailing middle-class standards. These poor households will have to occupy substandard housing units that are deteriorated, functionally obsolete, or overcrowded, or that exhibit some combination of those traits. Many such housing units will be within neighborhoods of concentrated poverty in central cities and older suburbs. The challenge is to remedy the adverse conditions in those areas as much as possible while avoiding the gentrification that simply shifts poverty to new areas.

That being said, urban policy needs to move away from the view of urban neighborhoods solely as problems to be solved. Urban areas offer many amenities attractive to skilled middle-class workers, and places that are reinvesting in such areas are discovering not only that they can ease the concentration of poverty but that a strong and vibrant urban core contributes to the overall economic health and quality of life in metropolitan areas. In this way, revitalizing urban areas becomes part and parcel of a strategy to better manage metropolitan growth.

Chapter 11

Large-lot housing in Franklin Township, New Jersey. Photograph by Anton Nelessen.

The Benefits of Sprawl

ALTHOUGH MANY CRITICS OF SPRAWL are reluctant to admit it, sprawl has dominated development throughout the United States for the past half century in part because it has provided most of its residents with real benefits they value. This chapter analyzes such benefits.

Many benefits of social actions are difficult to measure in terms comparable to other benefits, or even in terms comparable to the costs of the same activities. Some benefits—for example, purely psychological ones—are not measurable even in theory. For other benefits, their *incidence* is measurable—that is, the extent to which they actually occur. In this chapter, we analyze thirteen of these benefits. In many cases, however, no practical way exists to convert most such measurements into quantified estimates of economic value. Consequently, it is impossible to truly balance total benefits against total costs without making highly subjective judgments. Nevertheless, an exploration of sprawl's benefits in economic terms still holds value.

The first and perhaps most often cited benefit of sprawl is providing households with a lifestyle they desire. A key element of the American Dream—the ideal lifestyle sought by millions of households—is owning a detached, single-family home with a large yard in a safe neighborhood. Not everyone in our diverse society aspires to this lifestyle, but most Americans do.

In 1997, Fannie Mae conducted its National Housing Survey, which asked 1,652 people in all parts of the nation about their housing preferences. Seventy-one percent of those interviewed said that a "single-family detached house with a yard on all sides" was the "ideal" form of dwelling, compared to only 15 percent who considered the "single-family attached townhouse"—the second choice—as "ideal." Only 12 percent thought a multiple-family dwelling was "ideal."[1]

In 1999, the National Association of Homebuilders asked two thousand randomly selected households, "You have two options: buying a $150,000 townhouse in an urban setting close to public transportation, work, and shopping or purchasing a larger, detached single-family home in an outlying suburban area with longer distances to work, public transportation, and shopping. Which option would you choose?" Eighty-three percent of respondents chose the larger, farther-out suburban home.[2] Housing in sprawling areas consists predominantly of detached, single-family units, and most such housing is in the suburbs. In 2001, 67.1 percent of housing units occupied year-round in all U.S. suburbs combined were detached, single-family homes; 69.2 percent of all such units within metropolitan areas were in the suburbs.[3]

Demographic changes and changing preferences indicate that over the next twenty-five years more Americans may be seeking different housing choices (see Chapter 3). But helping households meet this basic lifestyle aspiration is probably the most important reason sprawl has been so popular for so long.

Home Price and Size

The ability to obtain the desired single-family home is at least in part due to the low cost of such homes in outlying areas. People seeking to buy homes long ago discovered that new housing tends to be less expensive when it is farther away from a region's center. Land located far out costs less than closer-in land, since the latter is more easily accessible to the many facilities already established in built-up areas. Many empirical studies have been made of the rate at which land and housing costs decline as distance from a regional center increases. They almost always confirm the wisdom of the home buyer's slogan "Drive until you qualify!"

A study analyzing home prices in Los Angeles in 1990 found that a one-mile increase in distance from the central business district would reduce the price of a home by 6 percent.[4] Since the average home price in the sample was $239,986, that would mean a drop of $20,879 per mile—a very high estimate. Another study of the Los Angeles area also found a strong correlation between home prices and the distance from downtown: houses farther away in straight-line miles were less expensive. However, when population density and distance from the Pacific Ocean were added to the equation, these factors outweighed any effect of the distance from downtown. An increase in distance from the Pacific Ocean of one mile would reduce the median home price by $4,363, or 1.92 percent.

In 1998, Robert Dunphy of the Urban Land Institute analyzed housing data from the Portland, Oregon, metropolitan area. He found a drop of 3 percent per mile in *small-lot prices* with greater distance from downtown Portland.[5] However, using *land prices per acre,* he found a decline of only about 0.9 percent per mile from downtown Portland to the urban growth boundary twenty-two miles away. When Dunphy used *finished home prices,* his analysis showed a decline rate of about 2.3 percent per mile.

These studies indicate that land and housing prices definitely fall with greater distance from most central business districts, unless some special influence—such as nearness to the ocean— overrides this effect. The studies show that housing prices fall somewhere between 1.5 and 6 percent per mile of distance from the urban center.

Is the benefit of lower house prices enough to more than offset the higher cost of commuting farther? A one-mile increase in daily commuting trips is 2 added miles per day, on each of 240 working days, or a total of 480 miles. If the commuter's car gets 20 miles per gallon and gasoline costs $1.50 per gallon, that is a marginal driving cost of 7.5 cents per mile for fuel plus, say, 2.5 cents for other operating expenses, for a total of 10 cents per mile. So the marginal fuel cost of driving another 480 miles is $48 per year. At an average speed of 25 miles per hour, the added time would amount to 19.2 hours. That time can be converted to a dollar value by assuming that the commuter values his or her commuting time at half the national average hourly wage of $15.52, which translates to $150 for the extra time per year. The total added driving cost would therefore be $198 per year. Dividing by a capitalization rate of 7 percent, it amounts to a capital charge of $2,829.

Whether it is worth that amount to buy a lower-priced home depends on the level of housing prices and mortgage terms in the particular region. As noted above, the cost of $198 capitalized at an interest rate of 7 percent amounts to a capital charge of $2,829. Assuming a thirty-year mortgage at 7 percent, the annual cost of one mile of additional driving could be offset by a home price that is $11,078 lower.[6] If that amount equals 1.5 percent of home prices in the region, then it is worth driving one more mile for any home priced at $738,583 or more. As of 2003, no U.S. region had home prices with a median that high. But if home prices in the region were to fall by 6 percent per mile, then one mile would gain a savings of more than the cost of that mile on any home of $184,645 or more. As of the first quarter of 2003, thirty U.S. regions had median home prices higher than that amount.[7] Thus, it is likely that sprawl provides a major benefit in lower land and home prices to residents of the many U.S. metropolitan areas that have relatively high home prices.

In addition to lower prices for homes farther out, sprawl allows people to own larger lots and build larger homes. The average lot size of a single-family, detached dwelling in a developed urban county is less than half the size of the average lot of the same type of dwelling in a developed area of a rural county. Suburban lot sizes are significantly larger than those in urban areas: 28.5 percent larger in developed portions, and 42.3 percent larger in undeveloped portions. Similar conclusions would apply to single-family, attached homes as well as multifamily and manufactured homes. More land provides more direct access to open space, more play space for children, more gardening space, and other benefits. Hence, increasing lot size adds somewhat to both the economic and psychological value of any home. However, as discussed in Chapter 4, this benefit may be offset by the costs of the loss of other types of open space, such as agricultural land and forests.

After attempting to estimate the economic value of the benefits of larger homes and lots, it becomes clear that such estimates would require so many arbitrary assumptions that the results would not be reliable. The earlier analysis of densities in this book does not specify dwelling unit sizes, and we have found no readily available data on variations in housing unit size by distance from the center of each metropolitan region. Therefore, although an advantage enjoyed by millions of households living in relatively far out, low-density settlements, this benefit cannot be quantified.

Public Schools and Crime

Another lifestyle benefit attributed to sprawl is that low-density suburban neighborhoods typically have better-quality public schools than do high-density central city neighborhoods. Insofar as this outcome exists, it undoubtedly arises mainly because the average socioeconomic status of residents living in low-density suburbs is much higher than that of residents living in high-density city neighborhoods.

Unfortunately, the enrollments of most big-city public school systems today are dominated by children from relatively low income, minority households that lack economic stability. For example, in 2002, the Chicago public school system contained 426,000 students attending nearly six hundred schools. About 85.3 percent of these children came from low-income households, 90.4 percent were minorities, and the average number of students leaving the school permanently during the school year was close to 25 percent. Among the 1.6 million students residing in the rest of Illinois, the median percentage of low-income students was 21.3 percent, the median percentage of minorities was 4.8 percent, and 12.4 percent of students left school during the year.[8] These figures illustrate the immense differences in student composition between many big-city public schools and schools in the surrounding suburbs.

School quality can be measured in part by examining academic test scores. The average academic achievement scores of low-income children are notably below those of children in schools with predominantly middle- or higher-income students, though many exceptions exist. In 2000, the average poverty rate in U.S. central cities was 18.4 percent, or more than double the average in the suburbs (8.3 percent). Thus, on average, city neighborhoods have greater poverty than suburban ones, so it is very likely that school achievement rates are higher in the suburbs than in cities, though few national data are available on that issue.

Another indicator of school quality is the amount of violence in schools. The National Center for Education Statistics reported that, for the school year 1996–97, the number of seriously violent incidents per one hundred thousand students was ninety-five for city schools, thirty-eight for urban-fringe schools, twenty-eight for town schools, and forty-five for rural schools. Clearly, city schools were much more violent than urban-fringe schools.

However, the superiority of schools in relatively remote, low-density neighborhoods is caused not by the far-out locations or lower density of those neighborhoods—that is, by traits defining sprawl —but by the particular groups of people who live there. Because of exclusionary local regulations and economic forces already described earlier in this book (see Chapter 10), the people living in far-out sprawling neighborhoods tend to have higher incomes, fewer children living in poverty, and lower percentages of minority-group households than people living in core-area concentrated poverty neighborhoods. Thus, when suburban residents extol sprawl for providing better-quality schools than those that prevail in big cities, they are essentially praising the effectiveness of the regulatory and economic barriers they have erected to prevent people who have those attributes listed above from residing in their areas. In addition, those exclusionary principles exact a cost on children in the urban school systems. Therefore, to consider superior schools in outlying areas a benefit of sprawl's defining traits is neither reasonable nor consistent with empirical data.

A similar association exists concerning levels of crime, especially violent crime, and neighborhood densities. Among the counties analyzed in detail in this study, crime rates in 1995 averaged almost 7,950 per 100,000 residents for urban center counties, 5,133 per 100,000 for suburban counties, and 3,521 per 100,000 for rural counties.[9] Clearly, other factors being equal, the more urbanized the type of county, the higher the crime rate it experienced. Does that make lower crime rates a benefit caused by sprawl?

Just as with the school-quality differences discussed above, low crime rates in the relatively remote neighborhoods created by sprawl are caused not by the *locations* or *low density* of those neighborhoods but by the particular *people* who live in them. Because of exclusionary regulations and other economic forces, people living in most sprawl-created neighborhoods tend to have higher incomes, fewer households headed by females, fewer children living in poverty, and lower percentages of Hispanic and other minority households than people living in core-area neighborhoods. In their landmark book *Crime and Human Nature,* criminologists James Q. Wilson and Richard J. Herrnstein state: "The possibility that neighborhoods have only a modest effect on criminality should not be surprising to readers familiar with the longitudinal studies of criminal careers.... Once we take into account the influence of constitutional factors, family socialization, and school experiences, there is not much left to explain, at least insofar as serious offenders are concerned."[10] Therefore, to consider low crime rates in outlying areas a benefit of sprawl's defining traits is neither reasonable nor consistent with empirical data. This result is confirmed by the fact that higher residential density by itself was *not* a statistically significant cause of higher crime rates in the analysis of central cities in 162 urbanized areas.

Transportation

Some urban economists have argued that sprawl has actually prevented some traffic congestion that would have arisen if new development had occurred in more compact, higher-density forms.[11] In 1990, commuting times for persons living in the suburbs and working in some other part of the same metropolitan area were 10 to 15 percent shorter than for persons living in central cities and working in some other part of the same metropolitan area. However, the advantage of lower average commuting times for suburban residents is constantly being eroded by increased automotive usage. From 1980 to 2000, the number of automotive vehicles registered in the United States rose by 1.2 for every additional person being added to the human population.[12] Furthermore, the average vehicle is being used more intensively than in the past. Vehicle miles traveled has risen 3.3 times as fast as the total population, and 1.9 times as fast as the number of vehicles. Consequently, the lower densities of outlying areas are being offset by more intensive use of vehicles, even in far-out suburbs.[13]

To test the hypothesis that commuting times are shorter for residents of sprawl than for people living in more dense areas, one study analyzed ninety-seven suburbs of Los Angeles in 2000. For each community, the average travel time to work among local residents was compared to the straight-line distance between the community's center and downtown Los Angeles. This analysis presumed that communities located farther from downtown Los Angeles are "more sprawling" and, hence, that their residents should have shorter average commuting times than the residents of closer-in communities, if this alleged benefit actually exists.

However, the analysis showed that more sprawl is associated with *longer* commuting times. To further test this conclusion, the ninety-seven communities were ranked in order of their distance from downtown Los Angeles and divided into five groups. Then the average distances and average commuting times for communities in each group were compared. The group farthest from the center, at an average distance of sixty miles, had an average commuting time of 32.9 minutes, and commute times fell slightly for each group thereafter, with the closest-in group having an average commute distance of eight miles and an average commute time of about 28 minutes.

These data show that more sprawl results in modestly *longer* commuting times. The group living farthest out is 7.4 times as far from the region's center as the group living closest but has an average commuting time only 17 percent longer than the latter. True, this study covers only one metropolitan area, so its results are hardly definitive. It suggests, however, that where jobs are highly scattered regionally, average commuting times are not closely related to residential distance from the regional center and that residents of highly sprawled areas are at a slight average commuting time *disadvantage* compared to those in more dense areas.

Some proponents of sprawl also claim that one of its benefits is the generation of less intensive traffic congestion than would occur in more compact development.[14] Because all types of land use are more spread out under sprawl development than under more compact development, the vehicles used by any given size population have more room in which to move freely than they would in more densely settled cities. As discussed in Chapter 8, an analysis of a Texas Transportation Institute congestion measure found that urbanized *area* density is indeed a statistically significant factor contributing to greater congestion in seventy-five U.S. metropolitan areas.[15] Thus it is reasonable to conclude that sprawl does provide lower traffic congestion, on the average, than more compact and therefore higher-density settlement patterns, although precise quantification of this benefit is not possible.

Defenders of sprawl have also argued that communities with low densities have lower total transportation costs than higher-density ones because public transit costs per mile are higher than private vehicle costs per mile. However, residents in low-density areas typically travel more miles each day than those living in higher-density areas. As noted in Chapter 8, the total cost of additional travel from 2000 to 2025 would be larger under the sprawl growth scenario than under the compact growth scenario, and more of those costs would also be borne by individuals since they are related to driving privately owned, single-occupancy vehicles. However, the travel cost savings from adopting the compact growth scenario, compared to the sprawl growth scenario, is extremely small in comparison to the total national costs of travel. The total savings *per day* achieved by shifting 25 percent of future growth into more compact areas over the next twenty-five years would be only 0.43 percent of the total cost per day of such transportation in 2000. In any case, it seems clear that sprawl does not provide society with any aggregate benefit of lower transportation costs.

Smaller Government Units

A defining characteristic of sprawl is the creation of many small governmental jurisdictions. The benefits of such small governments include stronger citizen participation and increased consumer choice regarding local public services and taxes. Urban economist Charles M. Tiebout contends that fragmentation of local government powers among many, relatively small local governments improves the welfare of society, as compared to having fewer, larger local governmental units. It does so by permitting households to have a wider range of choices among combinations of local tax rates, local "bundles" of public services financed with those taxes, and other local conditions.[16] This wider choice enables individual households to find combinations of those elements closer to their own preferences than they would have if they had only a few combinations from which to choose.

This argument has been reinforced by William A. Fischel's analysis of "homevoters"—that is, home-owning households who politically dominate most suburban governments.[17] Homes are the largest assets most households possess. Therefore, home owners are acutely interested in local conditions that influence the market value of their homes, including good-quality schools, safe neighborhoods, adequate parks and recreation, low traffic congestion, and the exclusion of most very poor households. Fischel regards this linkage of home owner interest in local conditions to maximizing home values as a major virtue of having many small local governments. This could reasonably be considered a benefit of sprawl.

However, such fragmentation generates a serious cost for society as a whole by permitting suburbs to adopt exclusionary zoning rules that aggravate the concentration of poor households within older, inner-core areas. The home-owning majority in many suburbs actively supports local government ordinances that make it difficult or impossible for lower-cost housing units to be built nearby. As a result, it becomes more difficult for low- and moderate-income households living in inner-core neighborhoods to find housing they can afford in the suburbs, thereby aggravating the ill effects of concentrated poverty in inner-core areas. This was the unanimous conclusion reached by the bipartisan Commission on Reducing Regulatory Barriers to Affordable Housing, which was appointed by Jack Kemp, secretary of the Department of Housing and Urban Development during the George H. W. Bush administration.[18] This outcome imposes significant long-run costs upon society as a whole.

It is not possible to reliably quantify the costs or the benefits of fragmentation. The total number of home-owning households in metropolitan suburbs with fragmented governance structures is much larger than the total number of poor households living in inner-core concentrated poverty neighborhoods. But the intensity of costs imposed on the latter by the adverse conditions found in their neighborhoods is probably greater per household than the intensity of gains derived by the former from fragmentation. And the long-run impact on society of those adverse conditions—including low skill levels, high crime rates, and high public service costs in many big cities—extends the costs of this condition far beyond its immediate effects on inner-core households.

In addition to giving home owners more choices, fragmenting local government powers among many relatively small municipalities magnifies the ability of individual citizens to influence their local governments, compared to the influence they would have if they lived in much more populous municipalities. It is almost self-evident that the average citizen of a town containing five hundred residents has a much better chance of persuading the local city council to adopt his or her views than the average resident of a city containing 5 million residents. This advantage of smaller size is indeed a major social benefit of fragmented government powers and is surely one reason Americans are so enamored of retaining such sweeping powers over local conditions at the municipal level rather than at higher levels. Moreover, in many cases, the potential ability to influence one's local government significantly encourages greater citizen participation in local government—one of the keystones of democracy. Therefore, stronger participation in local government is a social benefit of sprawl.

At the same time, such fragmentation can make it difficult for citizens to influence decisions that have a regional impact. And since many Americans may live in one jurisdiction, commute through another, and work in yet a third, they have interests in the metropolitan region as a whole that are not reflected by any single governing body. In addition, such fragmentation also leads to the exclusionary local policies discussed at length earlier in this chapter, with all their negative societal consequences. The ideal arrangement would be one in which local governance was fragmented enough to gain the benefit of citizen participation but also included some type of additional arrangements that prevented the exclusionary results that have such unfortunate consequences. (Trying to formulate such a dual arrangement is one objective of Chapter 12.)

Another controversial benefit of sprawl is its tendency to segregate citizens by income. The fragmentation of local government powers among many municipalities permits home-owning majorities in many communities to support exclusionary zoning, which reduces the percentage of local residents with incomes markedly below the median income. One reason localities adopt exclusionary zoning is the desire among most American households to live in neighborhoods where most of the other residents are a lot like themselves in income, social status, and often ethnic or racial composition. This desire for relative neighborhood homogeneity is by no means universal, but repeated surveys—plus the observed behavior of the population—have shown that most American households feel this way.

Whether this attitude is ethically appropriate in a democracy is controversial. Both legally and morally, American society has rejected public policies designed to create neighborhood *racial* homogeneity. Nevertheless, most Americans consider the racial composition of a neighborhood to be an important determinant of their willingness to live there.[19] The desire for relative *socioeconomic* homogeneity in neighborhoods is even more widespread. It is also encouraged, because many builders create large residential subdivisions in which nearly all the homes cost about the same and reflect the same basic designs.

At first glance, there seems to be nothing wrong with the view that "I would like to live in a neighborhood where most other households are a lot like mine and have similar views about what makes life in a community desirable." But applying this principle across all levels of society has unfortunate effects. It causes most very rich people to live with other very rich people, most middle-income people to live with other middle-income people, and most working-class people to live with other working-class people. Most of those groups probably regard these outcomes as desirable. But the same principle means that most very poor people live mainly with other very poor people in concentrated poverty neighborhoods. Experience shows that such areas do not provide healthy living environments, nor do they provide educational and training opportunities to the children there equal to those enjoyed by children in other parts of the same region.

Thus nearly universal application of the principle of socioeconomic neighborhood homogeneity excludes the poor from most residential areas, with many negative consequences for society. When combined with white reluctance to live in areas containing more than about one-third African Americans, this desire for socioeconomic homogeneity also concentrates poor African American households together far more intensively than poor white or Hispanic households. That intensifies the negative consequences of concentrated poverty for poor African Americans, who comprise a disproportionately large fraction of all households living in concentrated poverty neighborhoods.

Therefore, even though many Americans consider relative socioeconomic homogeneity among neighborhoods a benefit of sprawl, it contributes to results considered extremely undesirable for society as a whole.

Efficient Use of Infill

A final alleged benefit of sprawl is that leapfrog development makes more efficient use of land than solidly building up land at the suburban periphery.[20] As a large metropolitan area expands outward, sites once located at its edges become much more central. The sites that remain vacant can then be developed later at much higher densities without incurring the substantial costs of redevelopment. If the number of leapfrogged sites is large, the resulting overall savings in acquisition and demolition costs may be huge. Moreover, the whole metropolitan area becomes larger; so land costs near its center rise substantially. This makes it appropriate for land closer to the center to be developed with higher-density uses than were appropriate when those same sites were at the outer edge of development.

How important this sprawl benefit is depends on the percentage of once-peripheral land in a region that is initially "leapt over" by developers, the rate at which the region expands outward and thereby raises the densities at which it is most appropriate to develop skipped-over vacant sites, the costs of demolition, and the connection between skipped-over sites and the region's major transportation arteries. These factors all vary enormously from one region to another. Moreover, few reliable databases concerning any of these elements are available. Therefore, estimating the economic savings that a region reaps from having left some of its initially peripheral land skipped over by developers is impossible. As discussed in early chapters, leapfrog development also generates extra costs. Persons traveling to and from the area's outer edges must travel farther, roads and other infrastructures must be extended farther outward, and tax assessments on unimproved land are lower.

Conclusion

This chapter has reviewed the thirteen benefits of sprawl to determine whether they are truly the result of sprawl, how beneficial they actually are, and whom they benefit. The "true" social value of any benefit of sprawl can be evaluated by subjecting it to the following tests:

- Is this condition perceived by a large number of people to be a benefit?
- Is this condition actually caused by sprawl or by certain traits that are part of the basic definition of sprawl?
- Is this condition widespread enough in the United States to be socially significant?
- Does this condition have serious negative side effects or consequences that offset its benefits when considering its influence on society as a whole?
- Is this condition perceived by a large number of people to be a disadvantage?
- In sum, is this condition unequivocally a net benefit to society as a whole?

The results of subjecting the thirteen benefits to these tests are shown in Table 11.1. The thirteen benefits form the rows of the chart, and the six tests described above form the columns. Each cell states whether a particular benefit meets a specific test. Cells with results showing that a benefit is actually a "true" benefit are shaded. The brief judgments expressed in each cell are based on the detailed analyses of each benefit set forth earlier in this chapter.

Table 11.1 shows that five of the thirteen benefits of sprawl are indeed "true" net benefits to society as a whole. These five benefits are (1) lower land and housing costs on farther-out sites, (2) larger average lot sizes on such sites, (3) meeting widespread consumer preferences for low-density living, (4) providing households with wider choices of combinations of tax levels and social services than would occur under nonsprawl development, and (5) permitting greater individual citizen participation and influence over local government affairs than would occur under fewer and larger governments.

One benefit—total transportation costs lower than with more compact development—is definitely not a "true" benefit because sprawl probably has *higher* such costs. Another benefit—shorter commuting times—is also probably untrue for a majority of commuters living in sprawling areas. Three other alleged benefits— less intensive traffic congestion, larger home and room sizes, and more efficient use of infill sites—probably exist to some extent, but whether they occur at a great enough scale to be unequivocal advantages to society as a whole is unclear.

Better-quality schools, lower crime rates, and relatively homogeneous socioeconomic household composition in suburban areas definitely exist at a significant scale and are clearly perceived as benefits by millions of people. However, they also have serious negative consequences. Unfortunately, many communities achieve these benefits primarily by engaging in economically and socially exclusionary behavior. That behavior usually aggravates the involuntary concentration of very poor households in closer-in, concentrated poverty neighborhoods. Therefore, these three conditions cannot be considered unequivocally good for society or considered a benefit of sprawl.

The same criticism might be made against two other benefits of

TABLE 11.1
Are the Alleged Benefits of Sprawl True Benefits to Society as a Whole?

Benefits of Sprawl	Perceived as a Benefit by Many People	Actually Caused by Sprawl or Its Traits	Appears Widespread in Regions of the United States	Has Serious Negative Side Effects	Perceived as a Disadvantage by Many People	Unequivocally a Net Benefit to Society as a Whole
Lower land and housing costs	Yes	Yes	Probably	No	Partly	Probably
Larger average lot size	Yes	Yes	Yes	No	No	Yes
Larger home and room sizes	Yes	Not clear	Not clear	No	No	No, because actual extent of occurrence is not clear
Reflects low-density preferences	Yes	Yes	Yes	No	Unclear; some say not enough other choices are available	Yes
Shorter commuting time	Probably	Not clear	Not clear	No	Yes, because longer driving distances are involved	Not clear
Less-intensive traffic congestion	Only by a few people	Not clear	Not clear	No	Yes	No, because actual extent of occurrence is not clear

Lower overall transport costs	No	No	No	No	Yes	No
More efficient use of infill sites	Only by a few people	Yes	Not clear	No	Yes	No, because actual extent of occurrence is not clear
Neighborhoods with lower crime rates	Yes	Partly	Yes	Yes, partly caused by exclusionary behavior	Yes	No, because partly caused by exclusionary behavior
Better-quality public schools	Yes	Partly	Yes	Yes, partly caused by exclusionary behavior	Yes	No, because partly caused by exclusionary behavior
Greater consumer lifestyle choices	Yes	Yes	Yes	Yes; helps perpetuate exclusionary behavior	Yes	Yes
More homogeneous communities	Yes	Partly	Yes	Yes; based directly on very exclusionary behavior	Yes	No, because based directly on very exclusionary behavior
Stronger citizen participation and influence in local governments	Yes	Yes	Yes	Yes; helps perpetuate exclusionary behavior	No	Probably

Source: Downs (2002).

sprawl based on the fragmentation of governance powers: (1) a wider range of choice among combinations of tax and public service levels, and (2) greater citizen participation in and influence over local governments. However, these two conditions could also function without the adoption of exclusionary regulations: their benefit does not depend on exclusion. Therefore, neither wider choice of tax and public service combinations nor greater citizen influence is *inherently* harmful to low-income households. Moreover, both of these conditions are widespread and highly valued by millions of Americans, to the extent that they can be regarded as net benefits to society.

Surveying these results, is it possible to arrive at an overall conclusion concerning whether sprawl's benefits make sprawl generally superior to more compact forms of development? The answer is clearly, "No!" While sprawl obviously delivers some benefits, particularly to individual home owners, most of these benefits are balanced by significant social costs (as outlined in earlier sections of this book). However, in attempting to move toward more compact, efficient development, it makes sense to appreciate what has made sprawl attractive and to try to preserve at least some of those traits.

Chapter 12

Aerial photograph of Phoenix, Arizona. Photograph by Reid Ewing.

Developing Policies
in Response to Sprawl

WHAT PUBLIC AND OTHER TYPES OF POLICIES should be adopted in response to sprawl? This question is difficult to answer for several reasons. First, suburban sprawl is only one possible form of the American metropolitan growth process. However, it has been so dominant for the past half century that many Americans believe—erroneously—that sprawl is synonymous with metropolitan growth. Yet certain elements of the American metropolitan growth process that underlie both sprawl and all other potential forms of growth may be responsible for some of the negative effects attributed to sprawl. If so, policies responsive to specific drawbacks of sprawl may not counteract the negative impacts of those other elements of metropolitan growth.

Second, some form of peripheral growth in U.S. metropolitan areas has been inescapable in the past and probably will remain inescapable in the future. Over the past fifty years, large-scale population growth has forced many metropolitan areas to accommodate many more people. Rising real incomes have meant that more people have desired more space per household, and technical changes in transportation and communications have reduced the costs of living in lower-density settlements, thereby encouraging outward growth at lower densities than those that prevailed before

World War II. These forces together made some type of low-density outward expansion of U.S. metropolitan areas inevitable after about 1950.

The same powerful expansionary forces are still at work today and will probably remain so for the foreseeable future. In the 1990s, 93 percent of the nation's 335 primary metropolitan areas increased in population; they contained 96 percent of the nation's metropolitan area population and 78 percent of its total population in 2000.[1] Any policies responsive to sprawl must realistically address the need to continue accommodating those expansionary forces.

Another challenge in adopting policies is that sprawl clearly produces benefits as well as costs. It can be persuasively argued that, until now, sprawl's benefits have outweighed its costs. Future policies that reduce sprawl's negative impacts may also reduce its benefits. Therefore, the impacts of any policies pursued in response to sprawl on its positive benefits as well as its drawbacks must be considered before those policies can be recommended.

In addition, sprawl itself comprises several characteristics, meaning no "silver bullet" exists to "cure" it. Sprawl is defined as low-density, rapidly spreading urban development that leapfrogs out from an urban center. It is also marked by standardized development types that are strictly segregated from one another, creating reliance on automobiles. Some observers also say that fragmented governing structures and a lack of regional planning are defining traits of sprawl.

Clearly, devising effective policies responsive to sprawl is not a simple task. Such policies must address all of the characteristics described above. For this study, we used two policy tools—urban growth boundaries and urban service areas—intended to rein in the spread of development and presumably result in higher densities and less leapfrogging. Yet many other policies are necessary to achieve the vision put forth by proponents of smart growth or New Urbanism. In this chapter, we discuss some of the policy changes necessary to address both the fundamental traits of sprawl and the costs delineated in this book.

The compact growth scenario used the policy tools of urban

growth boundaries and urban service areas to estimate how much future sprawl might feasibly be shifted from where it seems likely to occur into areas closer to the center of each region. In this case, these techniques served primarily as a way to systematically conduct the cost analysis. The hypothetical boundaries drawn naturally could not take into account political realities, and they assumed a uniform impact on growth patterns. These tools are in use across the United States, and their real-world impact deserves a brief discussion. The adoption of urban containment policies (including growth boundaries, urban service areas, and greenbelts) grew steadily from the 1960s through the 1990s. A 1994 analysis found that such policies were in place in 45 percent of selected jurisdictions in mid-Atlantic states and in 29 percent of jurisdictions in western states, but were less prevalent in the South, the Northeast, and the Midwest.[2]

While, for this analysis, urban growth boundaries (UGBs) were defined at the regional level and were used to shift growth between counties, the majority of existing UGBs in the United States are drawn at the city or county level.[3] According to an analysis conducted by the Brookings Institution, such UGBs are most common in the West, particularly in California.

Metropolitan-wide UGBs have been drawn in just a few places, most notably in Oregon, where a state law passed in 1973 required boundaries for every metropolitan area. The Oregon Land Conservation and Development Act of 1973 required an inclusive process to determine future growth needs before the original boundary was drawn, and the boundaries are reviewed regularly (although they have not been changed significantly). These regional UGBs are not likely to be effective unless the state also adopts stringent limits on privately financed growth immediately outside each UGB and extending for a considerable distance beyond it. Otherwise, new development can spring up just outside the UGB, thereby defeating its purpose. This has been the experience in Boulder, Colorado, which created a boundary with a series of growth restrictions, including a greenbelt of preserved open space, while neighboring jurisdictions allowed unlimited growth. Satellite "bedroom" communities now surround Boulder, with residents crossing the greenbelt to get to work.

Urban service areas, or urban utility districts, contain growth by linking it to services provided by local government: roads, sewers, water, and the like. The best-known systems designate certain limited territories within a metropolitan area as the only places in which public funds will be used to finance sewage systems, water systems, roads, and other basic infrastructure supporting new development. This encourages private developers to locate their future projects within such service districts. This tactic was pioneered in the Twin Cities region (Minneapolis and St. Paul) of Minnesota and is being used at the state level in Maryland. Another way to achieve this same end is through adequate public facilities ordinances (APFOS), which restrict growth unless an area has enough roads, sewers, and so forth to service new development.

The setting of an urban growth boundary or service area does not automatically result in preserved open space outside the boundary or increased density within it. Urban boundaries work best if two other conditions are met: regions using them must also (1) significantly raise the allowable settlement densities within the boundary and (2) institute measures to preserve open space beyond the boundary. Both goals require policies or programs in addition to the boundary that are designed to encourage density and preserve open space —as well as the political will to actually carry through. All of these actions may involve transferring significant authority over land uses from local governments to a regional body or to the state government through state legislative action. A region that meets these three conditions can probably preserve a large amount of open space around its periphery free from urban development. This has been demonstrated over relatively long periods of time in Portland, Oregon; Lexington, Kentucky; and Miami, Florida.

However, two possible territorial obstacles reduce the likely effectiveness of such actions. First is that, over time, the actual growth of metropolitan regions tends to extend outward beyond their heretofore legally defined boundaries. Therefore, if the governmental changes described above apply only within the legally defined boundaries of each region, those changes will not control growth farther out that nevertheless greatly affects economic life within the region. The U.S. Census Bureau can readily redefine metropolitan area boundaries to capture such ongoing growth, but state governments cannot so easily expand the reach of their laws to encompass this growth—unless the laws are statewide to begin with (as was the case in Oregon). The second territorial obstacle arises when a metropolitan region includes land in more than one state. Then an effective growth-limiting policy may require coordinated legislation by two or more states—something rarely achieved in the United States.

Considering the number of environmental organizations and concerned citizens who would like to preserve more open space around the edges of their metropolitan regions, it is remarkable how few regions or states have adopted such policies. In almost all U.S. metropolitan areas, the amount of land used for urban purposes has grown much faster in percentage terms during the past twenty years than have the populations, households, or numbers of dwelling units in those regions. Even regions that have lost population (e.g., Pittsburgh) have nevertheless expanded their urbanized territories through low-density peripheral growth. Many critics of sprawl decry this seeming "squandering" of open land. Yet very few regions have successfully blocked continued outward low-density growth.

One reason is that most U.S. metropolitan regions still have large areas of relatively open space suitable for development immediately outside some or all of their settled territories. In fact, among the thirty-eight U.S. urbanized areas with more than 1 million residents in 2000, only seven—San Francisco, Seattle, Los Angeles, Miami, Pittsburgh, New Orleans, and possibly San Diego—can reasonably be considered hemmed in on all sides by water or mountains. Such widespread availability of nearby open land undermines claims by advocates of compact growth that drastic action must be undertaken to counteract an imminent shortage of open space. Only weak political pressure exists to preserve open space at the cost of making major changes in long-established laws and institutions.

As a result, efforts to carry out the regional exercises of power that are needed to stop most outward growth have succeeded mainly when associated with some type of environmental crisis. In Florida, the crisis was encroachment of urban development on the Everglades. In Oregon, it was similar encroachment on the open farmlands of the Willamette River Valley. In Kentucky, it was the widely shared desire to preserve the traditional horse-ranch country around Lexington. In Washington State, it was the desire to preserve open spaces between Puget Sound and the Cascade Mountains. Supporters of similar preservation policies in other regions have also claimed that environmental crises are imminent in order to rally political backing for the legislative changes necessary for their strategies.

Beyond Boundaries

As demonstrated throughout this book, urban growth boundaries and urban service boundaries would undoubtedly help control the costs of sprawl. However, these boundaries alone will not be able to direct growth. Dozens of other policy responses are being tried around the country to combat sprawl and control growth—for example, the Smart Growth Network has now published two books entitled *Getting to Smart Growth*, each with one hundred examples of policies that can lead to new growth patterns.[4] This chapter cannot hope to replicate that work but will discuss selected policy options as they relate to the traits of sprawl and the costs discussed in earlier chapters.

Preserving Open Space
The analysis in this book found that almost a quarter of projected land conversion could be avoided through urban growth boundaries or urban service areas without compromising growth or altering housing markets. The analysis also assumed that in undeveloped

areas under the compact growth scenario, much of the housing
would be built in clusters, a strategy that groups homes together
and preserves more open space. More compact growth would stop
"excessive" absorption of open land around the fringes of metropolitan areas that would be developed under sprawl. Proponents of compact growth claim that much of that land is now rich farmland
we need for agriculture, or environmentally sensitive land we need
to protect (e.g., wetlands and preserves for wildlife or endangered
species). Preserving more land from urban development would also
reduce water pollution from urban runoff into rivers, streams, and
bays. Such preservation would also make open spaces more accessible to urban residents. Techniques beyond growth boundaries used
to save land may include restricting development on certain lands or
transferring development rights.

Restrictions on Physically Developable Land

Certain territories within a locality, county, or state may be designated as not available for future urban development, at least in the
near future. Such territories may be (1) environmentally sensitive,
such as parts of the Florida Everglades; (2) federally owned, such as
the Department of Agriculture's land around Las Vegas; (3) owned
by an Indian tribe, such as land east of Scottsdale, Arizona; (4) used
as a watershed, such as land west of Interstate 280 south of San
Francisco; or (5) serving as habitat for an endangered species, such
as land along the Pacific Coast south of Newport Beach, California.
Many jurisdictions are also using innovative financing tools to purchase open space for preservation.

Transfer of Development Rights

States or counties may allow owners of certain vacant or agricultural
lands the right to sell future development rights to developers in
return for keeping those lands free from future urban development.
The purchaser of such rights can transfer the allowable densities to
other parcels closer in to existing settled areas, thereby raising the
densities permitted on those parcels. The objectives of this tactic are

to keep more outlying land as open space and to redirect future urban development onto closer-in sites at higher densities than would otherwise prevail there, while compensating farmers and ranchers so they can continue to work the land. Development rights can also be purchased outright by local jurisdictions to create conservation easements.

Economic Value of Open Space

In some areas, officials have calculated the economic value of preserving land for its "eco-services," such as water filtration or flood control. Considering this value can improve the chances of preservation by giving donors a larger tax write-off or by helping local governments meet other goals in addition to preserving open space.

SAVING INFRASTRUCTURE COSTS

The analysis conducted for this book found that more compact growth through boundaries would result in a combined cost savings for water and sewer service of $12.6 billion from 2000 to 2025 as well as a savings of $110 billion on road building. More compact growth would save both public and private funds because utility and road trunk lines serving growth areas would be shorter; more existing utility lines, streets, and schools could be used instead of always building new ones; and dwelling units would be smaller in higher-density settlements. This benefit is closely related to reduced absorption of open land, since that land would require the greatest expansion of infrastructure. Counties and municipalities are using several other techniques to lower the costs of providing such services and to ensure that developers pay a fair share of those costs.

Impact Fees

Localities often charge developers of new residential areas very high monetary fees for each new unit built or require them to provide or finance land, school buildings, parks, and other facilities for the community in return for the right to develop. This tactic aims to discourage new developments and help finance the infrastructure required to service new developments. Often, it also prevents any of the new dwellings from being affordable to low-income households. This tactic is widely used throughout the United States, though more to help finance new infrastructure and limit new growth than to make new growth.

Requirements for Adequacy of Public Facilities before Development
This tactic prohibits local or state governments from approving any new housing or other type of development unless the infrastructures needed to accommodate them—roads, sewers, water systems, and perhaps schools—have already been built or will be built at the same time as the developments themselves. Some areas, most notably Florida, require "concurrency" between infrastructure provision (roads, transit, water, sewer, solid waste, and parks) and property development to prevent new development from overloading existing infrastructures.

This tactic sometimes has the undesirable result of causing new development to spread out farther, because existing roads in already built-up areas are so congested that they are considered inadequate to serve additional development. When this happens, existing vacant infill sites served by those infrastructures cannot be developed. Developers instead shift their operations to more rural locations where traffic loads are still low, thus aggravating sprawl.

MAKING DEVELOPMENT EASIER AND MORE COST-EFFECTIVE
Our costs analysis found that a savings of $420 billion in real estate development costs can be achieved through more compact development. Compact settlements would broaden the range of available choices in housing styles and prices. Such settlements contain more multifamily dwelling units; more single-family attached units; and more publicly assisted units than typical sprawling subdivisions. This is because of the adoption of more innovative subdivision rules, more mixed-use zoning regulations, and more emphasis on affordable housing than under past sprawl policies.

These savings are a by-product of more compact development. Cities or counties can also deliberately save developers time and money through policies that encourage compact, mixed-use growth. Several techniques are being used across the country to change the rules of development to lower costs and encourage smart growth. (The issue of affordable housing for low-income residents will be discussed later in this chapter in the section on urban decline.)

Reducing Requirements for Expensive Building Materials

Many urban building codes require use of costly materials that could be replaced by equally satisfactory but less expensive newer materials. Cities should systematically review their building code requirements and remove all such unnecessary cost-raising elements.

Creating Accessory Apartments in Single-Family Homes

By allowing owners of single-family homes to add accessory apartments as a matter of right, cities could both greatly expand the supply of low-cost rental units and help elderly residents remain in their homes as long as they wish. This tactic was strongly recommended by the Commission on Reducing Regulatory Barriers to Affordable Housing in its report *Not in My Back Yard,* published in 1991.

Making Vacant Land Available for Immediate Development

Developers are often discouraged by the difficulty of assembling sizable parcels of vacant and developable land within large cities. City governments can use their powers of eminent domain to acquire many small parcels and group them together into much more usable large parcels. Getting such parcels zoned for the most suitable commercial, industrial, or residential use would remove another development obstacle. If developers realize that land is ready and entitled for immediate development with minimal delays, they would be much more likely to purchase it. City aid in either removing past pollutants or giving permission to develop sites without such removal would further encourage private development.

However, in many places, obtaining title to abandoned properties is a difficult and complex process that hampers the redevelopment of single lots. Some jurisdictions have established task forces, taken inventories, and changed ordinances to be able to bring such property back to productive use more quickly.

Streamlined Development Approval and Permission Processes

A major obstacle to private development in developed areas is the need for an entrepreneur to get project plans approved by dozens of different city agencies, each with different criteria for approval. Cities can streamline this process by allowing a developer to bring plans to one location where all relevant agencies are represented and where each can start work on the approval process immediately. In addition, some local governments are promising an expedited approval process for developments that meet a set of smart growth criteria. Others have changed master plans or zoning regulations to allow compact, mixed-use development "by right."

Early Public Involvement

Opposition by local residents can prove a time-consuming and costly barrier to development. To avoid such opposition, many local governments are using early and innovative public involvement processes to hear and address residents' concerns. Such processes may include charrettes—daylong workshops that bring together developers, traffic engineers, citizens, officials, and others to consider a proposed development and solve potential problems. Public involvement works best where local governments have already laid the groundwork with community planning and visioning processes.

REDUCING THE NEGATIVE FISCAL IMPACT OF DEVELOPMENT

Under the compact growth scenario, the costs of providing public services are projected to drop by $4 billion annually while revenues are expected to stay essentially the same. This would reduce the net fiscal deficit of the nation's towns, cities, and counties by nearly $40 billion annually by 2025. Reducing these costs is particularly important in central cities and some older, inner-ring suburbs, which have lost large portions of their former tax bases because of the outmigration of financially viable households and business to the suburbs.

The combination of shrinking tax bases and rising per capita expenditures in these areas puts a "fiscal squeeze" on local governments. Simply raising property and sales taxes motivates additional financially viable households and firms to move out, a situation that generates a self-reinforcing "downward fiscal spiral." The result is a lowering of both the quantity and quality of public services, including schooling, health care, and police and fire protection. Several strategies are being used across the country to reconfigure the tax situation in metropolitan areas to end this downward spiral.

Tax-Base Sharing
This policy tool requires each community to designate some part of its assessed value base, or of a stream of tax revenues, for inclusion in a regional pool, which is then divided among all participating localities by some formula. The assessed values or revenue streams to be included in the shared pool are only those added to each community subsequent to the date at which this arrangement is adopted by the state legislature. Such sharing reduces competition among communities for nonresidential properties to add to their tax bases and creates a fairer distribution of tax benefits from properties created in one community that impose costs on surrounding communities.

Tax-base sharing also reduces disparities among communities in providing local government services and facilitates sensible land use planning across a region with fragmented governance by making sure that benefits of development are more equally shared. In the Twin Cities region of Minnesota, this tactic applied to nonresidential property tax bases has notably reduced disparities among the localities included in the pool concerning their assessed property value per capita.

According to Myron Orfield, author of *Metropolitics*, tax-base sharing also enables local officials representing a majority of residents in the region to form a political coalition supporting such regional arrangements in the state legislature, even if representatives of localities containing a minority of the region's residents oppose those arrangements.[5] This possibility of a coalition can, in theory, overcome the ability of a minority of residents within a region to block the implementation of effective regional arrangements by refusing to participate in them voluntarily, even if a majority of the region's residents support those arrangements.

Provision by State Government of a Higher
Percentage of Local Revenue Needs
In some states, the state government offsets large disparities among local tax bases by providing a relatively high share of the costs of certain local services. In the 1992–93 school year, state governments as a whole paid for 45.8 percent of total spending on public elementary and secondary schools in the United States. In contrast, the state government of Hawaii provided 90.1 percent of total such spending in its state. The state governments of Alaska, California, Delaware, Idaho, Kentucky, New Mexico, North Carolina, Oklahoma, Washington, and West Virginia all provided more than 60 percent of such spending in their states. When a state government provides a high percentage of the funds needed to carry out some public service, the negative impact of sprawl on the ability of central cities and older suburbs to provide that service is reduced.

REDUCING TRAVEL COSTS AND EASING CONGESTION

The compact growth scenario found that Americans could travel 49.6 million fewer miles each day with an associated decrease of $24.1 million in daily travel costs due to more compact development achieved through growth boundaries and urban service areas. Both of these figures include increases in the transit component of overall travel costs under the compact growth scenario. However, as discussed, more compact growth may not have much impact on reducing peak-hour traffic congestion.

Among the policy goals most strongly advocated by critics of sprawl is reducing society's dependence on private automobiles for ground transportation. However, carrying out this policy will be difficult. Fifty years of automobile-oriented development means most Americans rightly see traveling by car as more convenient, more comfortable, safer, more private, sometimes less expensive, and usually much faster than traveling by public transit.

No matter how much transit travel is improved, getting a sizable number of Americans to shift out of private modes probably means making private driving much costlier or less convenient. The most obvious tactic is to place heavy taxes on gasoline sales to increase its price, as most other developed nations have done. But this practice has been decisively rejected by Congress repeatedly and by almost every federal administration; it appears to have very little chance of ever being adopted in the United States.

Another method to encourage the switch to transit is to increase automobile license fees and sales taxes. Singapore, for example, charges a huge annual fee just to make a potential buyer eligible to own a private vehicle, plus heavy sales taxes when the vehicle is purchased and high gasoline taxes when it is used. Denmark has a sales tax of more than 100 percent on all new vehicles. However, political support for this tactic is virtually nonexistent in the United States. Other tactics that encourage more efficient use of automobiles are more likely to be used.

High-Occupancy-Vehicle Lanes

High-occupancy-vehicle (HOV) lanes of various types, including high-occupancy-toll (HOT) lanes, reduce the number of private vehicles required to transport a given number of passengers during peak hours by encouraging people to carpool. Since traffic in most HOV lanes is relatively light, those who carpool can move faster during peak hours than those who do not. HOT lanes permit persons driving alone to travel in these fast-moving lanes if they pay a special toll to gain entry to them. This allows any driver who is in a big hurry to escape peak-hour congestion if he or she is willing to pay the toll, although it does nothing to alleviate peak-hour congestion for those not willing or able to pay. Revenues from HOT tolls are sometimes devoted to improving public transportation.

Peak-Hour Tolls

Charging high peak-hour tolls on major expressways and other commuter routes is designed to discourage enough people from traveling on the tolled roads during peak hours that traffic can move swiftly there. The charge has long been recommended by economists as a better way to ration scarce highway space. But so far this tactic has been blocked by politicians who recognize that most citizens do not want to pay rush-hour tolls for two reasons. First, they think such tolls are just another form of taxation on something they now receive without financial cost: driving during rush hours. Second, peak-hour tolls provide unfair advantages to wealthy commuters, who could travel swiftly, while less wealthy ones would have to travel at less convenient times or on less convenient routes.

Improvements to Transit Systems

Another method for reducing automobile dependency is to improve transit service, which is poorly available or nonexistent for most Americans. Just over half (57 percent) of American households report having public transportation service available, according to the U.S. Census Bureau's 2001 *American Housing Survey*. Some policy tactics are discussed below.

Rail transit systems. Building light rail or other rail systems can provide better accessibility to persons who cannot drive, help focus development around transit centers, and reduce air pollution. This tactic is becoming increasingly common in major metropolitan areas. Early light rail projects in Portland, Oregon, and San Diego, California, have been followed by new light rail investments in Denver, Miami, Salt Lake City, Dallas, Los Angeles, and several other cities. In all cases, substantial public subsidies other than fares have been needed to build and keep these systems running, and more than fifty projects are now seeking federal construction aid.

Special-lane busway systems. This tactic is more flexible than light rail and other fixed-track systems because buses can leave the fixed guideways and serve many different connecting routes without requiring passengers to change vehicles. Houston has established a large network of such busways.

Deregulating public transit delivery systems. This tactic seeks to make public transit more competitive by permitting individual jitney service, small-scale bus lines, use of nonunion drivers with lower pay, more taxis in each locality, private commuter bus service on unregulated routes, and withdrawal of transit service from routes with very low patronage. Ending current transit and taxi monopolies should improve the quantity and quality of transit service, thereby increasing ridership over the current low levels.

Encouraging More Compact Development

Perhaps the most effective way to reduce auto dependency circles back to the primary subject of this book: encouraging more compact development. Studies show that people who live in areas with higher densities and a mix of shops, offices, and other uses near home drive much less than their counterparts in traditional suburban subdivisions.[6] This is because they have several choices besides driving when leaving home, including taking transit, walking, or bicycling. Several policy proposals address this intersection between land use and transportation.

Transit-oriented development. Increasing development densities around public transit stops raises the number of persons living close enough to public transit stops (e.g., within half a mile) to walk to those stops. Focusing shops, services, workplaces, and other uses next to the transit stop makes it possible for residents to take care of daily life without using a car. Creating a string of TOD nodes reduces the number of automotive vehicle trips such persons make and increases the number of transit patrons. While relatively few places in the United States have instituted comprehensive TOD systems, they have greatly increased transit ridership, particularly for work trips, in Arlington, Virginia, and Portland,

Oregon. Many more metropolitan areas are beginning to build TOD communities.

Creating transit-oriented development is not easy. Local residents in communities currently served by transit stops often oppose increasing densities around those stops. Such resistance means plans to create transit-oriented developments sometimes end up not fulfilling their purpose.[7]

Bicycle and pedestrian infrastructure. Building bike paths, bike lanes, and pedestrian-friendly streetscapes makes it possible for people to use alternative trip modes for short errands, such as shopping, going to and from school, and even commuting. Some states, including California, Virginia, and South Carolina, have adopted "complete streets" policies to build and reconstruct every street as a complete transportation corridor that accommodates all likely modes. In other areas, developing bicycle or pedestrian infrastructure focused around certain areas or certain types of trips, such as through "Safe Routes to School" programs that install sidewalks, crosswalks, traffic calming, and other facilities to make it safe for children to bicycle or walk to school.

IMPROVING QUALITY OF LIFE

Many of the previous sections have touched on quality-of-life issues, such as traffic congestion and access to unspoiled natural areas. But some quality-of-life issues are less tangible. A complaint against suburban sprawl is that it lacks a sense of "place" and inhibits residents from feeling part of a community. Critics of sprawl want design changes that will allow more opportunities for people to meet, gather, and interact spontaneously; a mix of different land uses to shorten daily trip lengths and encourage personal interactions; and a greater sense of aesthetic pleasure and community.

Design is about detail, but a few tactics stand out.[8] For example, some communities are changing building codes to permit the construction of alleys behind homes and off-street garages, to reduce the dominance of cars in the streetscape. Because creating a memorable place is considered important, some developers are constructing new subdivisions around a central public place, such as a town square, often adjacent to a public transit stop. Grid street patterns encourage walking by providing more direct routes for pedestrians. Some places are even changing street construction codes to permit narrower and less heavily constructed streets, which discourage speeding and heavy commuting travel.

Crime and low-quality public schools have been the two of the most powerful quality-of-life factors motivating viable households and firms to move out of central cities and older suburbs. However, the sprawl-focused policy analysis presented in this book cannot present an in-depth discussion of the ways to improve schools and reduce crime. Smart growth's contribution to improving schools and crime rates may be the demographic changes suggested to decon-centrate poverty and bring greater income diversity to both cities and suburbs.

Reversing Urban Decline

As discussed throughout this book, the flip side of outward expansion is the decline of urban neighborhoods. While policies aimed at suburban areas may seek to contain growth, policies aimed at urban areas encourage new investment, at higher densities.

Tax Breaks

Property tax laws often discourage new development or rehabilitation because new or upgraded structures are soon assessed at higher levels. Providing tax abatements for initial periods and phasing taxes in over long periods can result in new improvements that increase property values in surrounding areas.

New Tax Structures

One tactic is to tax land and buildings separately, with much higher tax rates on land than on buildings in order to encourage development of vacant sites. Henry George suggested this policy long ago. Its goal is to pressure owners of vacant land to build by taxing the land at high rates but taxing the structures placed on the land at much lower rates. This system has long been used in Pittsburgh. However, switching a whole city or county to this system raises difficult transition issues.

Institutional Investment

Hospitals, universities, museums, medical clinics, and major public facilities are often located in inner-core areas surrounded by deterioration. To improve their ability to keep workers and recruit new ones, they should consider buying up nearby land and deteriorated structures, building new facilities or housing for their workers, rehabilitating older structures, maintaining local grounds and structures at high standards, and creating new parks and recreational spaces.

Revitalizing urban neighborhoods depends on improving the lives of the residents. Several actions related to compact growth contribute to achieving this benefit. Limiting outward regional growth would direct future growth pressures inward, driving up demands for land throughout existing built-up areas and increasing the pressure to invest in improving or replacing existing structures and building new ones. However, increased land prices might disadvantage existing poor residents, especially renters, since they would not benefit from home value appreciation. The acceptance of higher density in those neighborhoods would permit entry of many nonpoor households without having to displace all of the original poor residents, as long as a political commitment to maintaining lower-income housing exists. Higher density might also offset some of the impact of greater land prices on per-unit housing prices.

The creation of more affordable housing throughout the suburbs would permit some initial residents of concentrated poverty neighborhoods to move to suburban housing in nonpoverty neighborhoods, thereby improving their environments substantially. Such outmigration would also help make way for nonpoor in-migrants diverted from outward growth, who would help these neighborhoods attain a better balance of different income groups, thereby improving the local quality of life for the remaining poor households. Finally, direct investment in neighborhood revitalization would be needed to complete the positive life enrichment in these areas that was started by the other factors. If all of these changes were to take place substantially, the life chances of the initial residents in inner-core areas —including both those who had moved out and those who remained —would be greatly improved.

Many observers have concluded that reducing the negative impacts of concentrated poverty in inner-core neighborhoods requires reducing the poverty concentrations there.[9] Several strategies are under way both to help poor residents move out of such areas and to increase the number of higher-income residents moving into the areas.

Inclusionary Zoning

Residential developers creating a new housing subdivision over some minimum size (such as ten units) are required to include a minimum percentage of units—usually from 15 to 20 percent—priced to be affordable to households with incomes below the area-wide median income. The developers are usually compensated for this restriction by being allowed to build at a higher density than that for which the parcel was originally zoned. This tactic does not necessitate spending many public funds, since no direct subsidies are required to make these units affordable to relatively low-income households. It also mixes families occupying "affordable" units with those occupying market-rate units, rather than isolating the former in separate "projects."

The disadvantage of inclusionary zoning is that the initial buyers of the affordable units can reap a windfall gain if they are permitted to resell them at full market price; this would remove such units from affordable status. To prevent this, it is necessary to restrict ownership of such units to households with relatively low incomes, to place some administrative ceiling on the resale price that the initial owners can obtain, or to require that the initial owners remain in these units for some minimum time before they can resell at market prices. All of these remedies are administrative headaches. It is much more effective for an entire county, or even an entire state, to adopt such a program than for individual localities to do so. Montgomery County, Maryland, has used this program for several decades. As a result, several thousand more relatively affordable units have been built there than would have been without this program.

Housing Trust Funds

Money from real estate transfer taxes or other dedicated revenue sources is used to subsidize occupancy of housing by low-income households in suburban communities. Most state governments could impose a real estate transfer tax on all transactions within their boundaries without creating a "handicap" for home builders.

Numerical Targets

The state government, or some regional agency, can define numerical "targets" for the amount of low- and moderate-income housing that each locality should contain within its borders and can make certain state financial aids to local governments available in proportion to the governments' success at meeting those "targets." The basic idea is that each community in a region eventually should bear its "fair share" of providing housing for the poorer residents of the region's population.

Antidiscrimination Laws

Repeated studies by "testers" ostensibly seeking to buy or rent homes, as well as repeated statistical analyses of lending institution behavior, have shown that racial discrimination—though often subtle—is widespread in U.S. housing markets. Strengthening enforcement of antidiscrimination laws in housing and placing responsibility for such enforcement in a single regionwide agency run on a nonprofit public-private basis could help reduce poverty concentrations.

Overriding Zoning Boards

State laws can permit developers of affordable housing to override local zoning boards who "unreasonably" prevent them from building such units in their communities. The "snob zoning" law adopted several decades ago in Massachusetts was a forerunner of this approach. It permits developers who proposed to build low-cost units for low- and moderate-income households in areas that were zoned for multifamily residences to sue local zoning boards that refused them permission for such projects on grounds that clearly seemed exclusionary.

It is important to realize that certain other factors have much greater impacts on the life chances of persons living in low-income, inner-core areas than any policies connected with compact growth. The most important of these factors is the level of general prosperity in the overall U.S. economy and in the specific region concerned. In periods of the business cycle when labor markets are tight, unemployment is low, and incomes are rising, the quality of life of persons in these neighborhoods dramatically improves because incomes are much higher and more stable than during economic recessions. City governments are then also fiscally stronger and therefore provide better public services than in times of economic weakness.

Another crucial factor that influences the life chances of inner-core residents is the quality of public schooling available to them. For decades, the education profession has tried to improve the quality of inner-city public schools, compared to those in more affluent suburbs. So far, almost all attempts have failed despite enormous increases in public spending on big-city schools. Testing shows that students in these systems are still woefully behind those in most suburban systems. Surely a central reason for this situation is that so many students in big-city school systems come from economically and socially disadvantaged homes. Chicago public schools, for example, contain more than four hundred thousand students, over 80 percent of whom come from families poor enough to qualify for free lunches. Many of these students are from single-parent households, often headed by teenagers, who live in housing with abysmal conditions for studying and negative parental and peer-group pressures.

Under these conditions, it is hard to believe that any pedagogical innovations can overcome the ill effects of concentrating so many deprived students in a single system that becomes overwhelmingly dominated by them. That is why deconcentrating the poorest households in these neighborhoods to higher-income neighborhoods elsewhere should be a key goal of public educational and social policy. Doing so is one reason American society needs to create more affordable housing throughout the suburban portions of big metropolitan areas. This change could produce enormously positive social effects even if it were carried out in the absence of more compact growth, if it helped improve the quality of big-city public schools.

In reality, such general factors affect the welfare of inner-core residents much more significantly than whether a region has strong or weak growth boundaries or is willing to accept higher residential densities.

Encouraging Mixed Use

One fundamental trait of sprawl is segregation of uses, and a primary tactic of antisprawl efforts is finding ways to allow housing, businesses, retail shops, and other uses to coexist in close proximity. Research is showing that this trait is essential in providing transportation choice and creating a sense of place. A number of policy tools are being used for this purpose. Form-based zoning, for example, bases zoning decisions on the form of the buildings rather than on the buildings' current uses. So, as long as a structure meets height, setback, and other requirements, it can contain housing, shops, or an office. Another technique is to redevelop single-use developments, such as shopping malls, into mixed-use centers that include housing and other uses. Some jurisdictions are providing incentives for developments that put apartments over shops or are establishing programs to help people live close to where they work. As mentioned previously, transit-oriented development is also fundamentally a mixed-use strategy.

Providing Regional Governance

Most directly growth related problems in U.S. metropolitan areas are regional in nature, not local. But at present, the political and legal institutions with the greatest powers to respond to those problems are the federal government, which has traditionally favored sprawling development, and local governments, which have little motivation to act regionally. Local governments' most important such powers are control over land uses through zoning and building codes, and at least partial control over traffic arteries passing through their boundaries. However, local governments take far greater account of the impacts of their policies on their own resident voters than on persons living elsewhere in the region or on the region as a whole. In fact, no public officials within the typical U.S. metropolitan area are motivated to act for the benefit of the region as a whole.

The resulting inherent tension between the regional impacts of land use decisions and the purely local perspectives of those who make or regulate such decisions poses the single greatest challenge to effective planning and action within each region. Therefore, one key strategy for coping with growth-related problems effectively is to create organizations in a region that have both the legal responsibility and the political authority to coordinate land use and other related plans developed by individual localities and other government bodies. These organizations may have narrowly defined authority over a single domain of action—such as airports or water and sewer systems —or they may have much broader authority over multiple domains as they relate to land use.

A number of different types of regional arrangements have been tried or proposed as means of attacking the problems described above. These are briefly outlined below.

Functionally specialized agencies are the most commonly used regional arrangements, primarily for the mainly technical types of problems described earlier. Examples are the New York–New Jersey Port Authority, the Southeastern Pennsylvania Transit Authority, and the Metropolitan Sanitary District in the Chicago region. These agencies focus on one relatively narrowly defined set of activities that are mainly technical in nature and clearly regional in origin and impacts.

Voluntary confederations, such as the regional councils of government found in most U.S. metropolitan areas, are relatively easy to establish, primarily because they almost never have any real authority over any of their members. That lack of authority is their central drawback. Such organizations can rarely tackle controversial issues effectively, including any issues involving uneven allocations of resources among their members. But such agencies can draw attention to key issues and provide much relevant information about the issues to the public.

Public-private coalitions also lack authority, but they are excellent vehicles for calling attention to key issues and developing alternative plans for dealing with those issues—without choosing among those alternatives. Such coalitions, which can form without legislative authorization, can include broad cross sections of government, business, labor, academic, and religious leaders.

Federally created regional agencies are usually functionally specialized but can also have powers to carry out policies as well as money with which to do so. Examples are air quality control boards, which are set up in major metropolitan areas under the authority of the Environmental Protection Agency, or metropolitan planning organizations (MPOs), which are responsible for programming federal transportation funding. In theory, similar arrangements could be set up for all types of activities at least partly funded with federal money, including housing, health care, sewage treatment, and water systems. However, even these bodies are currently limited—for example, MPOs now control the spending of just 10 cents of every federal gas tax dollar generated within their boundaries.

Regional bodies with broad authority over several key functions must be established by state legislatures under the U.S. federal system. The most famous examples in the United States are in Portland, Oregon, and the Twin Cities region of Minnesota. The Portland Metro is a directly elected body with authority over surface transportation, sewer and water systems, and coordination of local land use plans. The Twin Cities Metropolitan Council has authority over surface transportation and major utilities plus advisory authority on low-cost housing. The Council is appointed by the governor. More recently, the State of Georgia established the Georgia Regional

Transportation Authority. The advantage of such bodies is that they exercise true regional powers over several closely related functions; hence, they can develop and carry out rational plans. The disadvantage is that it is extremely difficult to round up enough political support to get them established or to maintain their power.

Regional governments formed by merging municipalities and counties have been created in a handful of U.S. metropolitan areas, notably Indianapolis, Jacksonville, Nashville–Davidson, and Miami–Dade County. These bodies can be established by gaining consensus from city officials and county officials as well as by gaining approval from voters in the county involved. Their main advantage is that they encompass all local government functions with regionwide powers.

Contracts between separate governments can establish legally authorized bodies carrying out specialized functions throughout the territories of the entities that have signed the contract. This permits economies of scale not possible within smaller entities. A second key advantage of this arrangement is that it does not usually require constitutional changes or actions by state legislatures.

Conclusion

The preceding analysis shows that no single overall policy strategy concerning future growth is suitable to all, or even most, of America's many and diverse metropolitan regions. But policy makers may want to consider five major changes in existing institutions and behavior patterns that would be needed to make future growth enough to derive the benefits discussed in this book. Making these changes would require shifting significant influence over land use planning decisions from individual local governments to regional or statewide bodies.

The first change would be to make preservation of open space a priority, which requires adopting some kind of spatial limit on the outward expansion of development. Second, creating widespread affordable housing is fundamentally important and can be achieved in the suburbs by influencing decisions on local building codes and zoning. Third, public transit use should be encouraged through regional coordination and greater investment. Fourth, traffic congestion should be reduced through the use of HOV lanes, ramp metering, and other techniques. Finally, policy makers should substantially increase the amount of resources directed into revitalizing older inner-core neighborhoods in big cities and inner-ring suburbs. In the end, however, every region should create an overall growth-related policy strategy designed to fit its unique circumstances and conditions.

Appendix A

States Ranked by Sprawl Index

State	Rank	Sprawl Index (households)	Percentage of U.S. Household Growth Designated as Sprawl (%)	Percentage of all U.S. Household Growth (%)
Florida	1	16.0	12.8	10.3
Arizona	2	13.6	7.8	4.5
California	3	6.7	9.3	12.9
North Carolina	4	6.0	4.7	3.8
South Carolina	5	5.5	3.6	2.3
Nevada	6	4.7	3.0	1.9
Colorado	7	4.4	3.5	2.8
Maryland	8	3.8	2.7	1.9
Texas	9	3.4	6.2	11.2
Washington	10	3.2	3.4	3.6

State	Rank	Sprawl Index (households)	Percentage of U.S. Household Growth Designated as Sprawl (%)	Percentage of All U.S. Household Growth (%)
Illinois	26	1.2	1.4	1.6
Oregon	27	1.1	1.4	1.8
Arkansas	28	1.1	0.9	0.7
Montana	29	0.9	0.6	0.4
Louisiana	30	0.9	1.1	1.3
Utah	31	0.9	1.3	1.8
New York	32	0.8	0.9	1.1
Minnesota	33	0.7	1.1	1.7
Maine	34	0.6	0.5	0.5
South Dakota	35	0.6	0.4	0.2

State	Rank			
Missouri	11	2.8	1.9	1.2
Alabama	12	2.8	2.3	1.8
Pennsylvania	13	2.7	1.9	1.3
Georgia	14	2.7	3.4	4.3
Tennessee	15	2.5	2.6	2.7
New Jersey	16	2.4	1.6	1.0
Indiana	17	2.4	2.2	2.0
Ohio	18	2.3	2.3	2.3
Wisconsin	19	2.1	1.8	1.6
Michigan	20	1.8	1.9	2.0
Virginia	21	1.6	2.2	3.0
Alaska	22	1.5	0.9	0.5
New Hampshire	23	1.4	0.8	0.5
Mississippi	24	1.4	1.0	0.8
New Mexico	25	1.3	1.2	1.1

State	Rank			
Massachusetts	36	0.6	0.8	1.1
Kentucky	37	0.6	0.8	1.2
Hawaii	38	0.5	0.6	0.7
Oklahoma	39	0.5	0.6	0.9
Idaho	40	0.4	0.6	0.8
Rhode Island	41	0.4	0.3	0.2
Delaware	42	0.3	0.3	0.3
Connecticut	43	0.3	0.2	0.1
Iowa	44	0.3	0.4	0.5
North Dakota	45	0.3	0.2	0.1
West Virginia	46	0.2	0.3	0.3
Wyoming	47	0.2	0.2	0.2
Vermont	48	0.2	0.2	0.2
Kansas	49	0.1	0.2	0.2
Nebraska	50	0.0	0.1	0.4

Source: Center for Urban Policy Research, Rutgers University.

Appendix B

Counties Ranked by Sprawl Index (Top Thirty Counties)

Rank	County	1990 Households	1980–1990 Household Growth	Percentage of U.S. Sprawl 2000–2025	Major City	1990 Households	1980–1990 Household Growth
		(number)	(percent)			(number)	(percent)
1	Maricopa, AZ	807,560	48.2	5.06	Phoenix, AZ	369,921	29.9
2	Clark, NV	287,025	65.1	2.69	Las Vegas, NV	99,735	60.5
3	Palm Beach, FL	365,558	56.0	1.77	West Palm Beach, FL	28,787	8.3
4	Riverside, CA	402,067	65.5	1.72	Riverside, CA	75,463	23.8
5	Broward, FL	528,442	26.6	1.69	Ft. Lauderdale, FL	66,440	-1.7
6	San Bernardino, CA	464,737	50.6	1.64	San Bernardino, CA	54,482	27.2
7	Pima, AZ	261,792	37.8	1.40	Tucson, AZ	162,685	29.9
8	Arapahoe, CO	154,710	45.9	1.14	Littleton, CO	13,905	30.7
9	Wake, NC	165,743	55.6	1.10	Raleigh, NC	85,822	56.5
10	Seminole, FL	107,657	70.2	0.95	Sanford, FL	12,119	45.1
11	Snohomish, WA	171,713	42.3	0.88	Everett, WA	28,679	28.3
12	Pasco, FL	121,674	49.6	0.79	Dade City, FL	1,353	-35.6
13	Fort Bend, TX	70,424	76.8	0.79	Rosenberg, TX	6,428	14.3

14	Montgomery, TX	63,563	53.2	0.76	Conroe, TX	10,016	50.4
15	Manatee, FL	91,060	46.9	0.70	Bradenton, FL	18,871	52.6
16	El Paso, CO	146,965	36.3	0.69	Colorado Springs, CO	110,862	36.5
17	Utah, UT	70,168	19.9	0.65	Provo, UT	23,805	18.5
18	Solano, CA	113,429	41.0	0.63	Fairfield, CA	25,425	38.1
19	Lexington-Fayette, KY*	61,633	29.4	0.62	Lexington-Fayette, KY*	61,633	47.7
20	Lee, FL	140,124	69.8	0.61	Ft. Meyers, FL	18,144	25.9
21	Williamson, TX	48,792	95.7	0.60	Taylor, TX	29,381	12.9
22	Clark, WA	88,440	28.6	0.54	Vancouver, WA	20,138	7.1
23	Ventura, CA	217,298	25.8	0.52	Oxnard, CA	39,302	18.8
24	Anchorage, AK*	82,702	36.8	0.52	Anchorage, AK*	82,702	36.8
25	Montgomery, MD	282,228	36.2	0.51	Rockville, MD	15,660	8.7
26	Clackamas, OR	104,180	22.5	0.50	Portland, OR	187,268	17.9
27	Placer, CA	64,330	49.6	0.49	Roseville, CA	16,606	81.2
28	Sonoma, CA	149,540	29.8	0.49	Santa Rosa, CA	45,708	31.5
29	Greenville, SC	123,650	20.7	0.48	Greenville, SC	24,101	8.7
30	Butler, OH	104,830	18.7	0.46	Hamilton, OH	23,992	0.8

Sources: Projection data from Woods and Poole Economics Inc. CEDDS, 1998. Data interpretation by the Center for Urban Policy Research, Rutgers University.

* City-county government.

Notes

1. Introduction

1. Michael A. Pagano, *City Fiscal Conditions in 2003* (Washington, DC: National League of Cities, 2003), 1. National League of Cities homepage, http://www.nlc.org/home/.

2. National Governors Association and National Association of State Budget Officers, *The Fiscal Survey of States* (December 2003), x, http://www.nasbo.org/Publications/fiscsurv/fsfall2003.pdf; Pagano, *City Fiscal Conditions in 2003*, iv.

3. Pagano, *City Fiscal Conditions in 2003*, 8.

4. Arthur C. Nelson, "The Numbers of Forthcoming Growth," presentation at American Planning Association conference, April 2004, Washington, DC.

5. American Farmland Trust, *Cost of Community Services Studies: Making the Case for Conservation* (November 2002), http://www.farmlandinfo.org/documents/27757/FS_COCS_11-02.pdf.

2. Sprawl and Its Definition

1. John Delafons, *Land-Use Controls in the United States* (Cambridge, MA: Harvard-MIT Joint Center for Urban Studies, 1962), 10.

2. Dowell Myers et al., *The Coming Democracy*, Congress for the New Urbanism, San Francisco. Based on research by Dowell Myers, E. Gearin, T. Banerjee, and A. Garde, University of Southern California School of Policy, Planning, and Development. Available at http://www.cnu.org/cnu_reports/Coming_Democracy.pdf.

3. Robert Burchell et al., *The Costs and Benefits of Alternative Growth Patterns: The Impact Assessment of the New Jersey State Plan* (New Brunswick, NJ: Rutgers University Center for Urban Policy Research, 2000), 47–48.

3. Measuring Sprawl in the United States

1. Woods and Poole Economics, Inc., *CEDDS 1998* (Washington, DC: Woods and Poole Economics, Inc.; Rutgers University Center for Urban Policy Research, New Brunswick, NJ, 1998).

2. Robert Burchell, presentation S–139 "Smart Growth and Alternative Development Studies—What Do They Tell Us?" Monday, April 26, 2004. APA Annual Conference, Washington, DC.

3. http://www.bea.doc.gov/bea/regional/docs/econlist.cfm.

4. Land and Natural Resource Consequences of Sprawl

1. American Farmland Trust (AFT), 2002 *Annual Natural Resources Inventory* (Washington, DC: AFT, 2002). Available at http://www.farmlandinfo.org/farmland_technical_resources/index.cfm?function=article_view&articleID=29853.

2. U.S. Environmental Protection Agency (EPA), *Our Built and Natural Environments* (Washington, DC: EPA, 2001).

3. Farmland Information Center, *Why Save Farmland?*, http://www.farmlandinfo.org/documents/29493/Why_Save_Farmland_Color.pdf.

4. U.S. Environmental Protection Agency, *Our Built and Natural Environments*, 11.

5. New York City Department of Environmental Protection, "New York City's Water Supply System," http://www.ci.nyc.ny.us/html/dep/html/watersup.html.

5. Infrastructure Consequences

1. James E. Duncan et al., *The Search for Efficient Urban Growth Patterns* (Tallahassee: Florida Department of Community Affairs, 1989).

2. Robert Burchell, *Impact Assessment of the New Jersey State Development and Redevelopment Plan—Report II: Research Findings* (Trenton, NJ: New Jersey Office of State Planning).

3. Jonathon M. Harbor, "A Practical Method for Estimating the Impact of Land-Use Change on Surface Runoff, Groundwater Recharge, and Wetland Hydrology," *Journal of the American Planning Association,* 60, no. 1 (Winter 1994): 95–108.

6. Real Estate Development Costs

1. National Center for Public Policy Research, *Smart Growth and Its Effects on Housing Markets: The New Segregation* (November 2002), http://www.nationalcenter.org/NewSegregation.pdf.

2. This is gleaned from the discussion and tables on page 292 of Robert W. Burchell et al., *The Costs of Sprawl—2000* (Washington, DC: National Academy Press, 2002).

3. Robert Burchell and David Listokin, *Linking Vision with Capital: Challenges and Opportunities in Financing Smart Growth* (Washington, DC: Research Institute for Housing America, September 2001).

7. Fiscal Impact of Development

1. Robert W. Burchell, D. Listokin, and A. Pashman, *Regional Housing Opportunities for Lower-Income Households: A Resource Guide to Affordable Housing and Regional Mobility Strategies* (Washington, DC: U.S. Department of Housing and Urban Development, 1994).

2. Natural Resources Defense Council (NRDC), *Another Cost of Sprawl: The Effects of Land Use on Wastewater Utility Costs* (Washington, DC: NRDC, 1998).

3. Samuel Seskin, *Planned Growth Strategy* prepared by Parsons Brinckerhoff, 1999 (New York, NY) for the City of Albuquerque, New Mexico. Available at http://www.cabq.gov/council/pgs.html.

4. Grow Smart RI, *The Costs of Suburban Sprawl and Urban Decay in Rhode Island* (Providence, RI: Grow Smart RI, 1999).

5. Robert W. Burchell et al., *The Costs of Sprawl Revisited* (Washington, DC: National Academy Press, 1998), 56.

6. American Farmland Trust, *Cost of Community Services Studies: Making the Case for Conservation* (November 2002), http://www.farmlandinfo.org/documents/27757/FS_COCS_11-02.pdf.

8. TRAVEL AND CONGESTION

1. Because this survey is not comprehensive and only oversamples some metropolitan areas, the unit of analysis for this portion of the study differs somewhat from earlier impact chapters. Several adjustments were made to the analysis to make it parallel the analysis in other chapters. For more details, see Robert W. Burchell et al., *The Costs of Sprawl–2000* (Washington, DC: National Academy Press, 2002).

2. Reid Ewing and Robert Cervero, "Travel and the Built Environment," *Transportation Research Record* 1780 (2001): 87–114.

3. Catherine L. Ross and Anne E. Dunning, "Land Use Transportation Interaction: An Examination of the NPTS Data," in Federal Highway Administration (FHA), *Searching for Solutions: Nationwide Personal Transportation Symposium* (Bethesda, MD: FHA, October 29–31, 1997), 149.

4. Ewing and Cervero, "Travel and the Built Environment."

5. Lawrence D. Frank and Gary Pivo, "Impacts of Mixed Use and Density on Utilization of Three Modes of Travel: Single-occupant Vehicle, Transit, and Walking," *Transportation Research Record* 1466 (1994): 44–52.

6. Michael J. Greenwald and Marlon G. Boarnet, "Built Environment as Determinant of Walking Behavior: Analyzing Nonwork Pedestrian Travel in Portland, Oregon," *Transportation Research Record* 1780 (2001): 33–42.

7. Brian Saelens, James Sallis, and Lawrence Frank, "Environmental Correlates of Walking and Cycling: Findings from the Transportation, Urban Design, and Planning Literatures," *Annals of Behavioral Medicine* 25 (2003): 80–91.

8. Arthur C. Nelson, "Effects of Urban Containment on Housing Prices and Landowner Behavior," *Land Lines* (Lincoln Institute of Land Policy newsletter) 12, no. 3 (May 2000).

9. Todd Litman, *Transportation Cost Analysis: Techniques, Estimates and Implications* (Victoria, British Columbia: Victoria Transport Policy Institute, 1995).

10. Litman 1995.

11. See the work done by Samuel Seskin for Parsons, Brinckerhoff, Quade, and

Douglas in Robert Burchell et al., *The Costs of Sprawl—2000* (Washington, DC: National Academy Press, 2002).

12. This statement is incorrect according to the 2000 Census, Mean Travel Time to Work: All modes: overall commute time 25.5 minutes.

In metro areas: 26.1 minutes.
Outside metro areas: 22.9 minutes (rural).
Commute time breakdown within metro areas:
Inside central cities: 24.8 minutes.
Outside central cities but within metro areas: 26.9 minutes.

13. This principle was first defined by Anthony Downs in 1962 in "The Law of Peak-Hour Expressway Congestion," *Traffic Quarterly* 16, no. 3 (July 1962): 393–409. It is further developed in Anthony Downs, *Still Stuck in Traffic* (Washington, DC: Brookings Institution, 2004), chap. 5.

14. U.S. Environmental Protection Agency (EPA), *Characteristics and Performance of Regional Transportation Systems* (Washington, DC: EPA, 2004).

9. QUALITY-OF-LIFE CONSEQUENCES

1. Stuart A. Gabriel, Joe P. Mattey, and William L. Wascher, *Compensating Differentials and Evolution of the Quality of Life among US States* (San Francisco: Federal Reserve Bank of San Francisco, June 1996).

2. The following changes were made to Gabriel et al.'s variables before they were used in the county quality-of-life rating. The signs of the regression coefficients for five of the twenty-four variables were changed. States with (1) less sunshine, (2) higher rates of violent crime, (3) higher state and local property taxes, (4) more expenditures on higher education, and (5) more expenditures on welfare were associated with higher quality of life in Gabriel et al.'s regression equation. The signs of these variables were reversed when used in this analysis. Further, the influence of some variables (regardless of sign) on counties appeared to be too strong: the presence of a coast (within one hundred miles), better air quality (particularly low levels of carbon monoxide), a low number of hazardous waste sites, low student-to-teacher ratios, and significant funding for higher education and highways. The effects of these variables were reduced to one-quarter of their original influence.

In addition, several variables were eliminated from the analysis due to their seemingly inconsistent effects because the data were usually not reported at the county level: (1) the amount of federal land that existed statewide, (2) whether or not the state environmental protection laws were lenient, (3) the number of visits to national parks per one hundred people in the state, and (4) the number of visits to state parks per one hundred people in the state.

Other key variables were added: (1) wealth of the county, (2) share of the population age twenty-five and older with a graduate degree, (3) a cost-of-living index for the county, (4) future population growth, and (5) employment growth in the county. These additional variables, with the deduction of the four above, expanded the original variable set to twenty-six. Population growth and employment growth were found to exert too much influence and were reduced to one-quarter of their original effects.

3. Reid Ewing, Tom Schmid, and Richard Killingsworth, "Relationship between Urban Sprawl and Physical Activity, Obesity, and Morbidity," *American Journal of Health Promotion* 18 (September 2003): 47–57.

4. Lawrence Frank, M. A. Andresen, and T. L. Schmid, "Obesity Relationships with Community Design, Physical Activity, and Time Spent in Cars," *American Journal of Preventive Medicine* 27, no. 2 (August 2004): 87–96.

5. Brian Saelens, James Sallis, and Lawrence Frank, "Environmental Correlates of Walking and Cycling: Findings from the Transportation, Urban Design, and Planning Literatures," *Annals of Behavioral Medicine* 25 (2003): 80–91.

6. Eric A. Finkelstein, I. C. Fiebelkorn, and G. Wang, "State-Level Estimates of Annual Medical Expenditures Attributable to Obesity," *Obesity Research* 12, no. 1 (January 2004): 18–24.

7. Surface Transportation Policy Project, *Mean Streets 2002; Mean Streets 2000; and Mean Streets 1998* (Washington, DC: Surface Transportation Policy Project, 2002, 2000, and 1998).

8. U.S. Environmental Protection Agency (EPA), *Our Built and Natural Environments* (Washington, DC: EPA, 2001).

9. A. Seaton, W. MacNee, K. Donaldson, and D. Godden, "Particulate Air Pollution and Acute Health Effects," *Lancet* 345 (January 21, 1995): 176–78.

10. Todd Litman, "Transportation Cost and Benefit Analysis—Air Pollution Costs," in *Transportation Cost and Benefit Analysis: Techniques, Estimates and Implications* (Victoria, British Columbia: Victoria Transportation Policy Institute, June 2003), 510, http://www.vtpi.org/tca/tca0510.pdf.

11. Reid Ewing, Rolf Pendall, and Don Chen, *Measuring Sprawl and Its Impact* (Washington, DC: Smart Growth America, October 2002).

12. Robert W. Burchell et al., *Impact Assessment of the New Jersey Interim State Development and Redevelopment Plan, Report II: Research Findings* (Trenton: New Jersey Office of State Planning, 1992), 137.

13. Raymond W. Novaco, Daniel Stokols, and Louis Milanesi, "Objective and Subjective Dimensions of Travel Impedance as Determinants of Commuting Stress," *American Journal of Community Psychology* 18, no. 2 (1990): 231–257.

14. Tony Hiss, *The Experience of Place* (New York: Vintage, 1991).

15. Henry L. Diamond and Patrick F. Noonan, *Land Use in America* (Washington, DC: Island Press, 1996).

16. A. Nelessen, *Community and Housing Preference Survey* (Washington, DC: National Association of Realtors, October 2001), http://www.realtor.org/SG3.nsf/files/CommHousePrefSurvey.pdf/$FILE/CommHousePrefSurvey.pdf.

17. Constance Beaumont, *Historic Preservation* (Washington, DC: National Trust for Historic Preservation, 1996).

18. Jane Jacobs, *The Death and Life of Great American Cities* (New York: Random House, 1961).

19. David W. McMillan and D. M. Chavis, "Sense of Community: A Definition and Theory," *Journal of Community Psychology* 14, no. 1 (1986): 6–23.

20. Robert D. Putnam, *Bowling Alone: The Collapse and Revival of American Community* (New York: Simon and Schuster, 2000), p. 213.

21. Thomas H. Sander, "Social Capital and New Urbanism: Leading a Civic Horse to Water?," *National Civic Review* 91, no. 3 (Fall 2002): 213–234.

10. Sprawl, Urban Decline, and Social Policy

1. Bruce Katz, *A Progressive Agenda for Metropolitan America* (Washington, DC: Brookings Institution, May 2004).

2. Paul A. Jargowsky, *Stunning Progress, Hidden Problems: The Dramatic Decline of Concentrated Poverty in the 1990s* (Washington, DC: Brookings Institution, May 2003), 4.

3. Robert Burchell, A. Downs, S. Seskin, T. Moore, et al. *Costs of Sprawl—2000* (Washington, DC: Transit Cooperative Research Program, Transportation Research Board, National Research Council, Report 74, 2002), 373–439.

4. Robert W. Burchell et al., *The Costs of Sprawl—2000* (Washington, DC: National Academy Press, 2002), 406.

5. Bruce Katz, *A Progressive Agenda for Metropolitan America* (Washington, DC: The Brookings Institution, May 2004). Available at http://www.brook.edu/metro/publications/200405_katzgreenbook.htm.

11. The Benefits of Sprawl

1. Fannie Mae, *National Housing Survey—1997* (Washington, DC: Fannie Mae, 1998), 33.

2. National Association of Homebuilders, *What 21st Century Home Buyers Want: A Survey of Customer Preferences* (Washington, DC: National Association of Homebuilders, 2001).

3. *American Housing Survey for the United States, 2001,* Table 1C-1, U.S. Census Bureau, http://www.census.gov. The second-largest category of housing unit types in all suburbs combined consisted of attached, single-family homes (7.1 percent).

4. Denise DiPasquale and Matthew E. Kahn, "Measuring Neighborhood Investments: An Examination of Community Choice," *Real Estate Economics* 27, no. 3 (September 22, 1999): 389–424.

5. Robert T. Dunphy, *The Cost of Being Close: Land Values and Housing Prices in Portland's High Tech Corridor,* Working Paper Series No. 660 (Washington, DC: Urban Land Institute, 1998), http://research.uli.org.

6. The ratio of *annual* mortgage payments to the total amount of a mortgage for thirty years at 7 percent is 1 to 3.1328. Thus, commuting one mile less enables the buyer to support a mortgage larger by 3.1328 times $2,829, or $8,863. That would in turn comprise 80 percent of the additional home price that can be supported, if the down payment is 20 percent.

7. If the appropriate drop-off rate is 4 percent per mile, which is more likely than 6 percent, it would be worth driving another mile to buy any home worth

more than $277,000. Only eleven metropolitan areas had median home prices above that amount in the first quarter of 2003. Data from the National Association of Realtors, *Real Estate Outlook: Market Trends and Insights* 10, no. 7 (July 2003): 18–19.

8. Education Committee of the Commercial Club of Chicago, *Left Behind* (Chicago: Commercial Club of Chicago, 2003), 6, 39.

9. The data on crime used here were prepared by the Federal Bureau of Investigation and taken from a CD published by the U.S. Census Bureau, *USA Counties 1998* (Washington, DC: U.S. Department of Commerce, 1999). This CD shows the rate of serious crimes per one hundred thousand residents for all U.S. counties for which such information was available.

10. James Q. Wilson and Richard J. Herrnstein, *Crime and Human Nature* (New York: Simon and Schuster, 1985), 291.

11. Peter Gordon and Harry W. Richardson, "Are Compact Cities a Desirable Planning Goal?" *Journal of the American Planning Association* 63, no. 1 (Winter 1997).

12. Vehicle registrations involve some duplication among states, so they slightly overstate the actual vehicle population. Even so, since 1980, the nation has been adding more than one automotive vehicle to the vehicle population for every one person we add to the human population.

13. U.S. Census Bureau, *Statistical Abstract of the United States: 1999* (Washington, DC: U.S. Census Bureau, 1999). Available at http:www. census.gov/prod/www/statistical-abstract-us.html.

14. Gordon and Richardson, "Are Compact Cities a Desirable Planning Goal?"

15. Anthony Downs, *Still Stuck in Traffic* (Washington, DC: Brookings Institution, 2004), chapter 3.

16. Charles M. Tiebout, "A Pure Theory of Local Expenditures," *Journal of Political Economy* 64 (October 1956): 416–24. Tiebout later wrote several other articles expanding on this original idea.

17. William A. Fischel, *The Homevoter Hypothesis: How Home Values Influence Local Government Taxation, School Finance, and Land-Use Policies* (unpublished manuscript, February 7, 2000).

18. Commission on Reducing Regulatory Barriers to Affordable Housing, *Not in My Back Yard* (Washington, DC: U.S. Department of Housing and Urban Development, 1991).

19. For evidence supporting this statement, see Douglas Massey and Nancy Denton, *American Apartheid* (Cambridge, MA: Harvard University Press, 1993), chaps. 5 and 6.

20. Richard B. Peiser, "Density and Urban Sprawl," *Land Economics* 63, no. 3 (August 1989): 193–204.

12. DEVELOPING POLICIES IN RESPONSE TO SPRAWL

1. Data from the U.S. Census Bureau's Census 2000 PHC-T-3 Ranking Tables for Metropolitan Areas: 1990 and 2000. Table 1: Metropolitan Areas and Their Geographic Components in Alphabetic Sort, 1990 and 2000 Population and Numeric and Percent Population Change, 1990 to 2000.

2. Rolf Pendall, "Residential Growth Controls and Racial and Ethnic Diversity: Making and Breaking the Chain of Exclusion" (PhD dissertation, Department of City and Regional Planning, University of California, Berkeley, 1995).

3. Rolf Pendall, Jonathan Martin, and William Fulton, *Holding the Line: Urban Containment in the United States* (Washington, DC: Brookings Institution, August 2002).

4. ICMA/Smart Growth Network, *Getting to Smart Growth: 100 Policies for Implementation* (2002); and *Getting to Smart Growth II: 100 More Policies for Implementation* (2004), http://www.smartgrowth.org/library/articles.asp?art=870.

5. Myron Orfield, *Metropolitics: A Regional Agenda for Community and Stability* (Washington, DC: Brookings Institution Press; Cambridge, MA: Lincoln Institute of Land Policy, 1997).

6. Lawrence Frank, "Obesity Relationships with Community Design, Physical Activity, and Time Spent in Cars," *American Journal of Preventive Medicine* 27, no. 2 (August 2004): 87–96.

7. Hank Dittmar and Gloria Ohland, *The New Transit Town* (Washington, DC: Island Press, 2004).

8. For a discussion of these and other New Urbanist policies, see Peter Katz, *The New Urbanism* (New York: McGraw-Hill, 1994).

9. For example, Anthony Downs, *Opening Up the Suburbs* (New Haven, CT: Yale University Press, 1973); National Advisory Commission on Civil Disorders, *Report* (New York: Bantam Books, 1968), chaps. 16 and 17.

References

Beaumont, Constance. 1996. *Smart States, Better Communities.* Washington, DC: National Trust for Historic Preservation.

Burchell, Robert W. 1997. *South Carolina Infrastructure Study: Projection of Statewide Infrastructure Costs 1995–2015.* New Brunswick, NJ: Center for Urban Policy Research, Rutgers University.

Burchell, Robert W., William Dolphin, and Catherine C. Galley. 2000. *The Costs and Benefits of Alternative Growth Patterns: The Impact Assessment of the New Jersey State Plan.* New Brunswick, NJ: Center for Urban Policy Research, Rutgers University.

Burchell, Robert W., Anthony Downs, Samuel Seskin, Terry Moore, Naveed Shad, David Listokin, Judy S. Davis, David Helton, Michelle Gall, and Hillary Phillips. 1998. *The Costs of Sprawl Revisited.* Washington, DC: National Academy Press.

Burchell, Robert W., David Listokin, and William Dolphin. 1994. *Development Impact Assessment Handbook.* Washington, DC: Urban Land Institute.

Burchell, Robert W., George Lowenstein, William R. Dolphin, Catherine C. Galley, Anthony Downs, Samuel Seskin, Katherine Gray Still, and Terry Moore. 2002. *The Costs of Sprawl—2000.* Washington, DC: National Academy Press.

Burchell, Robert W., and Harvey S. Moskowitz. 1995. *Impact Assessment of DELEP CCMP versus STATUS QUO on Twelve Municipalities in the DELEP Region.* Report prepared for the Local Governments Committee of the Delaware Estuary Program, Philadelphia. August 15.

Delafons, John. 1962. *Land-Use Controls in the United States.* Cambridge, MA: Harvard-MIT Joint Center for Urban Studies.

Downs, Anthony. 2002. "Have Housing Prices Risen Faster in Portland than Elsewhere?" *Housing Policy Debate* (Fannie Mae Foundation) 13, no. 1: 7–31. Available at http://www.fanniemaefoundation.org/programs/hpd/v13i1-downs.shtml.

Environment Colorado Research and Policy Center (ECRPC). 2000. *The Fiscal Costs of Sprawl.* Denver: ECRPC.

Landis, John D. 1995. "Imagining Land Use Futures: Applying the California Urban Futures Model." *Journal of the American Planning Association* 61, no. 4: 438–57.

Muro, Mark, and Robert Puentes. 2004. *Investing in a Better Future: A Review of the Fiscal and Competitive Advantages of Smarter Growth Development Patterns.* Washington, DC: Brookings Institution Center on Urban and Metropolitan Policy.

Nelson, Arthur C., Rolf Pendall, Casey J. Dawkins, and Gerrit J. Knaap. 2002. *The Link between Growth Management and Housing Affordability: The Aca-*

demic Evidence. Washington, DC: Brookings Institution. Available at http://www.brook.edu/es/urban/publications/growthmanagexsum.htm.

Real Estate Research Corporation (RERC). 1974. *The Costs of Sprawl: Environmental and Economic Costs of Alternative Residential Development Patterns at the Urban Fringe.* Vol.1, *Detailed Cost Analysis;* vol. 2, *Literature Review and Bibliography.* Washington, DC: U.S. Government Printing Office.

"Smart Growth Index." 2003. *USA Today.* Sprawl Index article is available at http://www.usatoday.com/news/sprawl/main.htm.

Smart Growth Network. 2002. "About Smart Growth." Available at http://www.smartgrowth.org/about/Default.asp?res=1400.

Victoria Transport Policy Institute. 2002. *Transportation Cost and Benefit Analysis: Techniques, Estimates and Implications.* Updated June 2003. Available at http://www.vtpi.org/tca/. (A 1995 version of this paper was used for the analysis in this book.)

Index